OTHER BOOKS BY KAZIMIERZ BRANDYS

A Warsaw Diary

Paris, New York: 1982–1984

Kazimierz Brandys

PARIS, NEW YORK; 1982-1984

Translated by
Barbara Krzywicki-Herburt

 Random House New York

Originally published in France in Polish as *Miesiace 1982–1984*
by Institut Litteraire, S.A.R.L., Paris, 1984.
Copyright © 1984 by Kazimierz Brandys

Library of Congress Cataloging-in-Publication Data
Brandys, Kazimierz.
Paris, New York: 1982–1984.
Translated from Polish by Barbara Krzywicki-Herburt.
1. Brandys, Kazimierz—Biography—Exile.
2. Authors, Polish—20th century—Biography—Exile.
3. Paris (France)—Description—1975–
4. New York (N.Y.)—Description—1981–   . I. Title.
PG7158.B632A367   1988   891.8′58703 [B] 88-4369
ISBN 0-394-54492-7

Manufactured in the United States of America
Typography and binding design by J. K. Lambert
9 8 7 6 5 4 3 2
First American Edition

June 1982

Sunday. Paris. A damp afternoon at Père-Lachaise cemetery. Old women hold session along the park benches, and birds, mostly robins and blackbirds, flit from tree to tree above the graves. Chopin's is in section number eleven. We follow the map given to us by the cemetery guard, lose our way, and suddenly come upon a marble sarcophagus covered with flowers. Under a red-and-gold strip of ribbon, several letters are visible: F. CHOP . . . We stop. What a profusion of flowers! Then it occurs to me that Chopin's grave, in the photographs I've seen, was built of white stone, whereas this one is dark. And where is Clésinger's sculpture? I push the ribbon aside and read the remaining letters carved in marble: F. CHOPPIN.

So this isn't it. The Chopins never spelled their name with a double p. We are approached by a balding, round-faced man in glasses, with a book under his arm. He has guessed what we're looking for. "Please allow me, I come over here every day and I know by heart where everyone's buried." A Frenchman. His short legs and small feet in tennis shoes carry him swiftly; I can barely keep up. M. drops behind. The Frenchman tells us that this is where he spends his vacations. He works for an insurance company and comes to the cemetery every day bringing his lunch, to enjoy the tranquillity until closing time. "No summer resort provides as much solitude and quiet. You should also visit the cemetery of Montmartre! Complete peace. It's an older cemetery, with fewer visitors. I recommend it."

He escorts us to Chopin's grave: a light, narrow monument, just inches away from those on either side. How little space there is! As closing time approaches he hurries us from Musset to Balzac, to Nerval, Apollinaire, and Géricault. The Frenchman has the air of a host escorting visitors through his estate. At Sarah Bernhardt's grave, which resembles a bunker, he stops and gently strokes the gravestone. "*Pauvre Sarah,* nobody brings her flowers. . . ." Beside the plot of Marcel Proust are those of his parents and his brother, Professor Robert Proust, and his brother's wife who died in 1953. The air is stifling. The old women get up from the benches and move in the direction of the exits. We can hear the guard's whistles announcing closing time.

My impression is by and large not what I expected. Everything is concrete and stone, divided into sections; you feel you're walking down the streets of a miniature city, with graves instead of houses.

The mood is less melancholy, less pastoral than at Warsaw's Powazki cemetery. Powazki has more space, more dead leaves on its overgrown graves. Here, surrounded by an urban neatness, one is somehow conscious of the fact that fame is subject to the democratic law of death.

Someone once asked me why I didn't attend the funeral of a mutual acquaintance. "I'm opposed to funerals: They'll never drag me alive to my own," I said. In those days I felt it was necessary for a man to be witty.

I have never associated a cemetery with anything but worms and bones. There is no soul drifting over it. It's a place with tombstones and monuments. I feel no response or vibration. But a week ago I stood staring for a quarter of an hour at a narrow townhouse on Ile Saint-Louis, once the home of Daumier, unable to tear myself away. Once I had walked up the stairs to the door of Proust's apartment near the Place Madeleine to touch the doorknob with my hand. To me the dead are not in cemeteries. They've remained in the houses they lived in, and it is there, not at their graveside, that I feel their presence.

Thursday, I had a talk with Madame Brunau, head of the Cité Internationale des Arts, where we've been staying since the beginning of May. It is a modern, horizontal building not far from the Hôtel de Ville. Several hundred people, mostly musicians and artists, live in its five stories of identical studios consisting of a room for work, with high windows and a sleeping section, and a tiny kitchen and a bathroom. Upstairs, there is a small television hall, in the basement a series of concert and art exhibit rooms. The tenants are an international group of artists. Swedes, Argentinians, Yugoslavs, Dutchmen, Italians . . . also there are Asian couples with children in baby carriages. I was placed here on the recommendaton of the French Ministry of Culture and, through the efforts of various friends as well as strangers, was assigned a studio for two months on the second floor with a view of Notre Dame. In the course of the conversation with Madame Brunau on Thursday, our stay was extended for another two months, until September 1. For a hundred days, I will have a roof over my head. We had flown in from New York on April 19. After half a year's interruption—in New York I merely took notes—I can now write again.

The interior, the furniture (a simple one-drawer table, two sleeping sofas covered with plaid blankets), and the rich foliage outside the windows, remind me of our summer vacations in Kazimierz or Sopot; the houses provided by the Writers' Clubs in Poland had a similar decor. But here, above the trees, are the two towers of Notre Dame, their color changing with the time of the day: from the white of dried bones at noon to the crab-shell pink of sunset. Through the leaves I can see cars gliding along the bank of the river.

Warsaw . . . New York . . . Paris . . . Where next? Should I describe everything that happened, and still continues to happen, everything that was destroyed? During our final months in Warsaw, before we left, I felt it was the diary that kept me going: I didn't know how to live outside its rhythmic flow. I tried to justify this with arguments fabricated ad hoc. In my New York notes, I wrote, "It's often said that life is a novel. I'm writing my diary to find out whether my life is a novel." It may have been true. But today I make a different point. I write my diary because it's the only thing that helps me survive slipping out of the temporal order.

Late one evening, eight days after arriving in New York, our telephone rang. M. answered it. I was in the next room. After a while I heard, "Oh, my God . . ." and I put down my book. She listened as someone spoke at the other end. Then I heard her voice again, the same muffled, "Oh, my God . . ."

About two weeks later, I woke her up in the middle of the night. I asked her if she was absolutely certain we were still alive, if it was possible this was all a dream. What if our plane from Warsaw had crashed into the ocean, and we had been living an existence that had retained some traces of our former lives, but was actually the hereafter? What if we were dead to our former selves? Maybe that's what dying is like: For a while, there's a semblance, an illusion of continuity, and weeks, or even months pass before we come to understand we've been transformed into another incarnation. I asked her not to turn on the light. I suggested we lie in the dark, concentrating as hard as we could. Maybe we would remember. "But what are we supposed to remember?" she asked, half asleep. "How we crashed into the ocean," I explained.

Such talk frightened her. But to me, more improbable than my calamity at sea was this: While I was falling asleep on my sofa in Queens, on that very same night in Warsaw, doors were being broken down with crowbars and my friends were being removed by force from their homes. The same friends we had spoken to the day before we left Warsaw. Everything had been interrupted, everything had fallen apart. Our former life seemed vague, a thing that would have to be reconstructed out of many scattered fragments in the early morning hours.

///

One day at noon, I surfaced onto the street from a subway station. Cold winds swept across Manhattan. In the sun, the vertical skyscraper prisms glistened like icebergs. I had submitted my application for a three-month relief grant up on the twelfth floor of one of the tall towers. In another that gleamed like pale amber, I had taken one of the eight elevators to the twenty-fourth floor, where in a gold-carpeted office I was admitted by an official with a hearing aid. I assured him I'd be ready to go to South Carolina in exchange for a year's grant. During the intermission between the two appointments, I sat over a cup of coffee served in a waxed paper cup at McDonald's. I was prepared to make the most bizarre decisions. Had someone offered me a teaching grant in Alaska, I would have accepted without hesitation. Since

I'd been cut off from my life and, with two suitcases, thrown into another time zone, on the opposite side of the globe, it made no difference to me whether I would teach Eskimos in the North or black students in the south. I had but one thought in my mind: nine hundred dollars per month. That was the amount I needed to be able to support M. and myself.

//

I was returning home having been awarded the three-month grant. The more permanent arrangements did not seem to be working out. The office clerk had hinted at some vague possibilities and spoke of a blind millionairess in Palm Beach looking for a reader. Walking along Fifth Avenue, I heard a familiar melody, probably a tune by Gershwin. At Rockefeller Center, a mass of ice skaters swirled in the sun. I stopped at the railing among a small group of onlookers. I noticed that only I seemed to be finding this sight extraordinary. To the other casual spectators it was commonplace. A woman standing beside me with a small poodle turned in my direction, saying something. I nodded in agreement, without actually understanding her. Her words seemed to be coming from her throat, up through her nose, merging in a sound like that made by an automobile horn. After one month, I'd become convinced I understood their language less and less each day, and calmly awaited the moment when it would stop reaching me altogether, and I would plunge into the blessed indifference of the deaf.

The first news reports spoke of the seizure of power by the army, mass arrests, the cutoff of communication from and inside Poland. Soon, more detailed information became available: tanks and armored cars in the streets, efforts to break the resistance of factory workers and miners, the first lists of names of the interned. The newsmen emphasized the speed and precision of the operation that took place on the night of December 12–13. Almost the entire leadership of Solidarity was seized in a few hours and placed in camps. There was not a single battle in the streets. The next day, American television showed the first pictures from Warsaw: a woman on the sidewalk, with a shopping bag. In a coat and fur hat, falling to her knees and calling for help, and a man, also on his knees, kissing the pavement. Then a helmeted police detachment, stopping pedestrians and cars. The streets in the photographs were already covered with snow. The Warsaw television announcers were dressed in military uniforms and read the news items without looking directly at the camera.

The American press estimated the number of arrests at tens of thousands. Among the names mentioned at the top of the list, in addition to Walesa, were Kuron, Michnik, and Lipski. *The New York Times* reported a false piece of information about the death of Tadeusz Mazowiecki and about the serious beating of Adam Michnik by the police. In time, some facts were confirmed. At the Wujek mines, stormed by the police, five miners had died. Jerzy Zielinski, who worked for the weekly *Solidarnosc*, committed suicide. Many married couples were arrested and weeping children were taken from their mothers; special police squads involved in the roundups were issued crowbars to force the doors open. On the list of the arrested, the names of Halina Mikolajska, Jacek Bochenski, and Wiktor Woroszylski came up repeatedly. Andrzej Kijowski was also mentioned. They were put in trucks, sometimes in their pajamas and nightgowns, and then taken by helicopter to camps and prisons. John Darnton, the Warsaw correspondent of *The New York Times*, mentioned my brother Marian as one of the arrested. All day long I telephoned Paris, asking my friends and acquaintances for help. The French Ministry of Culture and the International PEN Club intervened, but later it turned out that the source of Darnton's information was gossip circulating around Warsaw. News of this kind may have been spread in order to be proven false later on and undermine the credibility of true accounts.

//

In New York, in January, I made a list of the nightmares tormenting me in the early morning hours. There were eight: never being able to return to my apartment in Warsaw; the triumph of Russia over all of Europe; teaching at the University of Ohio; not sending enough packages to Warsaw; being old; not knowing where in New York I can have the broken zipper on my trousers repaired; the death of Poland; and uncertainty about the existence of God.

Paris. A heat wave in June. At the Cité des Arts, directly above us, lives a Japanese man, a pianist. As long as he plays classical compositions, he does not disturb my writing. But when he switches to avant-garde music, I can't write, think, or read. In the afternoon, the studio, hot as a summer veranda, has a vacationlike atmosphere. We walk around half-naked or stretch out, thumbing through the newspapers. M. has drawn the shades. "The important thing," she says, "is for us to feel temporary, in transit. In the end, we've always gone back." The clerk at the prefect's office, checking our passports, asked, *"Vous êtes de passage?"* M. smiled. "Oh yes. Naturally." Our visitors' permits were extended.

Sunday at the Kunderas. The conversation revolves around Polish and Czech affairs, the means of survival available to a captive nation, whether there are alternatives to violence. I talk about the uprisings that took place in Poland under the Russian occupation, and the differences not only between Czechoslovakia and Poland but also between the sections of Poland, one occupied by Russia, the other by the Austro-Hungarian Empire. In the second half of the nineteenth century, the rule of the Habsburg monarchy, which allowed limited national representation, influenced Polish mentality quite differently than the way of life in the territories taken over by Russia. For two hundred years, since the original partition of Poland by Russia, any thought of cooperation between or even coexistence of the two nations has been stubbornly and consistently rejected in favor of force and oppression. Under these circumstances revolt has seemed necessary. But the temptation to comply and the spirit of rebellion always appear to coexist, and have generated very individual conceptions of national existence. Patriotic resistance has not been the only Polish response. The denial of national independence has also taken its toll.

The Kunderas came out of Czechoslovakia with two suitcases, leaving behind them in their apartment their furniture, books, manuscripts. At first they called their stay abroad "a vacation": They thought they would be returning to Prague quite soon. "How long have we been here," Kundera asked his wife. "Seven years."

After leaving the Kunderas, it was impossible to take a bus on the Boulevard Saint-Germain because thousands of pacifists were holding a demonstration. They carried posters and effigies and shouted slogans. Some posters were anti-American; one such poster was carried by a group of lesbians and homosexual men who also waved their own organization's flag. Many people were walking with their children, with flowers in their hands and colorful balloons. Taped songs by Grassens and Montand played over loudspeakers, artistic groupings symbolizing peace rode on truck platforms. Teachers, artists, and university staff, beautiful women and men with intellectual faces marched in the streets. *"Pour la guerre: non, non, non! Pour la paix: oui, oui, oui!"* Some of the posters protesting the installation of American nuclear rockets depicted Marx and Lenin, Stalin and Mao, although their inclusion in the protest march did make one wonder, considering the vast numbers of their victims. Also curious was the absence of slogans expressing solidarity with Poland. And not one protest against the invasion of Afghanistan. Some people in the parade were dancing, holding each other's hands. The weather was sunny and warm, the women wore low-cut summer dresses showing off their brown, suntanned shoulders; confetti was being thrown from passing trucks.

Observing all of this from the sidewalk, I couldn't help thinking to myself that while a hundred thousand people were marching through the boulevards of Paris protesting United States armaments, Soviet nuclear rockets were being aimed at France.

///

Everybody has the right to act in self-defense when threatened. In the West, it has recently become fashionable to defend what threatens you. A French or German progressive liberal finds moral and political justification for the bloody acts of terror in Paris or Munich, while firmly denouncing the presence of American military bases in Europe and elsewhere. He has sympathy for the forces that try to undermine his country from within, at the same time as he condemns those who improve its defense against attack from the outside. There's a kind of masochism in the humble tolerance that every other Parisian journalist shows the fantastic designs aimed against his far from imperfect world. One gets the impression these journalists are ready to agree with anyone who would find murdering them a pleasure. This runs contrary to biological instinct, and shows profound self-doubt. Anyone who hates them, they believe, must be better than they are. Leszek Kolakowski in his book *Can the Devil Be Saved?* expresses the view that the ability to doubt and question oneself is a main characteristic of European culture. This is certainly true of Western Europeans.

During the parade of the pacifists on Boulevard Saint-Germain, my wallet with my Polish Writers' Union card and some old receipts was stolen. Since then, I've been carrying a small edition of the Gospel of Saint Luke in my pocket. I am waiting for someone to steal that.

//

In the middle of the night I had a dream, and then I woke up. In the dream I was putting my parents to bed. Wrapping warm blankets around them I told them to sleep safely, and not to worry about anything. They dozed off, grateful. I tiptoed to the door, and then turned around to see if they had fallen asleep. They were covered up so well I couldn't see their faces. When I leaned over to touch them, the blanket collapsed. They weren't there, although the covers had held their shape. Ripping the blankets off the bed, I shouted I had to see them. A voice said I had to choose the one I wanted to see. I screamed, "My father!" Then I saw M. Sitting in a chair, she pointed to the empty armchair beside her. Hanging over it was a crumpled velvet smoking jacket. My father had just risen from that chair, only to vanish. M. was looking at me with a smile, as if trying to explain by her glance something obvious and simple.

A dream remembered in detail is a rare thing. Here I intended to describe its final moment, which I kept secret from M. when I told her about the dream the morning after, and which I had omitted from my notes. A hand had suddenly reached out from behind the chair railing. A fat, dirty hand, unfamiliar, tightening over M.'s mouth.

///

In America, I slept badly. I often lay for hours in the early morning with the growing awareness that we were lost and would perish. I visualized how we would have to spread a mattress under the Queensboro Bridge the day after spending our last penny and losing the roof over our heads, and felt relief in this possibility: to die quietly from cold and hunger, among the glittering towers of the city, and not have to sign any more petitions, compile biographical data, or fill out any more questionnaires. One sentence often repeated with friendly smiles by our New York friends and acquaintances intrigued me. "Don't worry, in this country no one can perish." I waited impatiently to see in what way the truth of these words would be confirmed in our own case.

In the second part of the day I sometimes had a few free hours. Pretending to read, I would devote myself instead to the task of remembering. Those were active, energy-filled hours. Reconstructing the past in a detailed, intense, sometimes laborious fashion, and at the same time surrendering to images, feelings, and sounds previously hidden in a crude state of memory, I reached nearly occult states of awareness. Sometimes the reexperience of random events in the past seemed infinitely more profound than the former reality.

I recalled scenes from my childhood. I reconstructed love gestures and moments of ecstacy. By concentrating on one scene, I was able to add imaginary details and invent words I had been unable to utter at the time. These experiences were pleasurable and, during my first few months in New York, provided a good deal of solace.

There were many people at that time who were helpful to us. Their concern expressed itself not only in words. Our old and new friends assisted us in practical matters, took care of us. But their help had to end one day, since they did, after all, have their own lives to live, their own problems. Feeling as I had since mid-December as though I were in an airplane crashing into the ocean, I didn't believe that permanent help was a realistic possibility.

//

This describes someone I know very well: There's in him as much goodness that he doesn't fulfill, as evil that he doesn't commit.

July 1982

From this Parisian square, I see the street as two receding lines of fawn-gray trunks (a common color in nature: the color of mice, elephants, and earth). Above the sidewalks, on either side, run three parallel motifs, one on top of the other: awnings, shutters, and roofs. The awnings are navy blue, dark green, and the shade of faded amaranth, and are edged in silver or gold. The letters printed on them are white or lemon yellow. The black, vertical lines of the shutters extend the black ironwork design of the balconies, reminding me of lines and notes on a sheet of music. The white walls, visible at intervals behind the trees, look ash gray in the shade, and creamy when illuminated. Everything here serves to enhance the balance of the vertical and horizontal areas. The street runs straight to its destination, the riverbank and the bridge. It dates back to a time when human reason still prevailed in cities.

//

On Saturday after midnight, we were returning home from dinner with friends, and we drove across the Latin Quarter, which was still full of traffic and lights. Groups of people were leaving the restaurants, laughing; the automobiles along Boulevard Saint-Michel were honking their horns, unable to move in the traffic. Two women sat in the front of our car and three men in the back. Behind them, in the luggage area, under the back window, squatted a third woman; whenever the car speeded up, she laughed. Of the six people in the car, one was returning to Poland the following week, three in a month and a half, and two were undecided. We were not drunk, but not totally sober either. Somebody said, "When you get back, it'll be probably after the uprising." Somebody else added, "Who knows, maybe before." The woman in the luggage area asked us not to forget the medicine for her cousin, recently released from Goldapi prison camp. Someone told a joke about a monk hearing the confession of a militiaman. The car moved slowly down the boulevard, the weather was warm, many people were sitting on café terraces around small tables set closely together.

I can remember all the topics that came up in the conversation that night: the Pope's visit to Poland; the strike of the television actors; the rationing of goods and black market prices; the analogies between the Israeli armed raid in Lebanon and Pilsudski's Kiev campaign; Fibak's, the tennis champion's, estimated earnings; the December 13 night session of the Polish National Council at the Belvedere Palace; the shortages of clothing and shoes; the Polish Primate's conciliatory tendencies; the publication in *Tygodnik Powszechny* of a poem by Wiktor Woroszylski, now a prisoner in a camp for the interned; somebody's divorce.

Our conversation, lasting several hours, had, first at the dinner table and later in the car, a tone which to me was intimately familiar. A shrewd observer, with a knowledge of Polish, would have seen in us a group of people using a code—a code maintained in order to fend off that disaster of which we all felt a part. One of us might have said, "How awful! It's impossible to find a good French wine anywhere in Warsaw!" Who would miss French wine in a city where finding tea or a pair of shoes is a problem? The lack of shoes or of medicine, the growing mortality rate, the prisoners held in camps inside Poland, and increasing poverty—makes a complaint about the lack of French wine seem like a simple cynicism. But it is self-directed irony. Humor of this type serves to keep despair at bay; it is a protest against aberrant behavior.

Over the centuries, the Polish language has been altering its means of defense against a loss of national sanity: from Wespazjan Kochowski's laments, through the rationalistic sarcasm of Krasicki, to the heart-strengthening writings of

Sienkiewicz. *Sursum Corda!* The memory of our greatness will lift us out of our spiritual prostration. Half a century later, Witkacy tried to fend off the approaching disaster with his boy-genius eloquence.

Faulkner once said he was puzzled in his youth by the words he had read on the first page of Sienkiewicz's *Trilogy*. I wonder whether *Sursum Corda*, "strengthen your hearts," wasn't inadvertently translated by the American translator as "cure your hearts."

What does it mean to think, to write, to speak the Polish language? Should you let it be, or adapt it instead to a universal form, understandable to others? After December 13, I would wake up in the middle of the night on my sofa bed in Queens, and there, to my right, were the sleeping pills, and to my left, the window (six flights up). I felt I should choose one of these two alternatives. But I also felt it would be unfair to at least two people. The other one being the friend who had extended us her hospitality. I tried to figure out what could get me out of the depression overwhelming me. A university job? What a terrible prospect! I'd have to lecture in English, whereas I can think only in Polish. Working in another field would separate me from my mental substance, formed by layers of Polish associations and reactions. It would be utter torture. To make a living by writing and earn enough to be able to sustain a peaceful, fairly comfortable existence, would be possible only if my books became international best sellers translated and published in foreign languages, and this was highly unlikely, to say the least. I've never once had the desire to read any of my books in their translations, which bore me from the very first page, and read as though written by somebody of no interest to me. Nothing can free me from the prison of my own language, because my prison bars are within. That which is called *language* doesn't consist merely of the words we speak; it is the voice of our common consciousness, the tone we assume when speaking to our prison guards. It isn't only a memory—it is a neverending reply to destiny.

"You'll be back, just wait and see," writes a young woman from Warsaw in a letter to someone who has remained in France, "and I hope our planes don't cross in flight, because, after the war's been won, I'm taking off for the South Seas to bask in the sun."

Ah, Warsaw humor . . . *ironia polonica* vis-à-vis life.

//

If I've said that captivity drives you mad, then, recalling the idyllic Sunday parade on Boulevard Saint-Germain, where they carried the portrait of Josif Vissarionovich, I'm tempted to say that freedom makes you stupid. I hope the reader can forgive me for both these blasphemies.

//

In Queens, and on subway trains, I heard every language under the sun. Spanish, Russian, Hindi, Yiddish, Ukrainian, Italian, Chinese . . . on the busses and in Manhattan, the majority of sounds were purely American, nasal and vibrating, in which I couldn't distinguish the individual words. On certain days in January, I would walk down Park Avenue, or down Fifth Avenue, in the direction of Sixty-sixth Street. The glass towers plunged from the sky to the sidewalks. They looked triumphant in their daring. Some seemed fluid, their walls streaming down to the asphalt. One green, with white stripes, another dark and transparent, with the neighboring buildings reflected in its glass walls. The older skyscrapers, built of metal and concrete, with columns and porticos at the entrance, were also awe inspiring, with their facades stretching almost too high: Renaissance down below, then over fifty stories of concrete, and finally, stuck on the top, a small secession-style private residence right out of Konstancin. Near Fifty-seventh Street, the light and straight icebergs out of some superplanet rise to the sky. A city imagined by a child.

The colorful towers of Manhattan, reaching with such lunatic courage, are doubtless a victory for mankind. But victory over what? There's one now in planning I've heard, that will be 220 stories high. From a roof restaurant on the top of a silver-white skyscraper, I spotted a helicopter flying down below, looking no larger than an insect. Still lower down, I could see the Statue of Liberty, the size of a figurine in a gift shop. The restaurant guests, on the other hand, did not look too different from people you would pass on a street in a small town in Poland, such as Dytom or Pzeszow. Perhaps these sky-reaching specters are not a victory for mankind, but a victory over mankind. They have surpassed and out-

distanced man. Next to them, he seems mediocre, an ana-
chronism. At times I had the impression that the crowds
inhabiting Manhattan suited quite well its five- or seven-story
structures, while the skyscrapers were built by different
creatures.

///

The New York Subway has a bad reputation. It is foul and
dirty, covered with crazy graffiti, the train races forward with
a wild roar. Down in the subways people sell narcotics; they
commit murder and rape. But this I wasn't afraid of. Inside
the rushing subway car I felt safer than in a Manhattan street,
because the sitting or standing passengers were motionless
and I could see each face at close range, as if magnified. I
could look and listen. And smell. Here steamed the bowels
of the city. Mixed in color, reaking of sweat and deodorants.
Painted transvestites sat next to young Hassidic Jews with
side curls; across from me, a black woman in a leopard coat
and a white turban was reading *Ecology of Modern Science*. Once
I had missed seven stops observing a small Chinese woman
while she trimmed the fingernails of her husband with scis-
sors, leaning thoughtfully over his hand with its long, thin
fingers.

So—I was thinking—it can work after all. This very difficult thing. They've done it. Any place else, knives would
be flashing. Here, something has jelled, the multiplicity of
languages, rites, and races are integrated into one living entity.

Notes for future use: American literature has a moral

purity. It has taken the side of the weaker, of those being killed. Nineteenth-century Russian literature defended the Russian serf and spoke out against his grim lot. In the era of lynchings, American writers tried to save the soul of America.

///

What was it I was afraid of in New York? The distances. But not the geographic ones. The distances between the words I had within me and the environment that had given them their origin. Also, I was afraid that I would never get away from here, while they in Poland would never get out of prisons, or escape their privation. Afraid that we would soon be but a memory to each other, remembered only in dreams. Afraid that they wouldn't believe the anguish I suffer in this foreign land. Or that I would never again sit in my old armchair by the window to write. I was missing my furniture, as well as my friends.

And yet, I must admit I wasn't in a hurry to return to Poland. Poland frightened me no less than being cut off from it did. I was aware of the fact that even my manuscript would not be safe there, because at any moment they can break down your door, with or without a search warrant. I wasn't longing to go back. Nor did I miss my former life in Poland. Not even the walks in the Saski Garden, or the Warsaw streets, racially pure to the point of boredom. Once, walking in a multilingual crowd in Manhattan, I remembered the words of a professor from Boston who had returned for a visit to Poland after thirty years. "You've lost your minorities, gotten rid of what was left of the Jews. You will have trouble with your culture."

It wasn't nostalgia that was consuming me. Yet I rejected in panic the thought of never returning. Returning home and seeing our old janitor, Mr. Pawlak, sitting in the courtyard on his little stool, I always felt certain no harm could come to me. I was home. And yet, only there did I so often experience a total loss of the will to live. There were days when a feeling of total senselessness would overwhelm me. On such days, I struggled to find words that would defy senselessness, that would allow me to argue in favor of life. I think that for a quarter of a century I had been doing nothing but that; and perhaps more than anything else, I was obsessed in New York by the fear that the words would not come, that senselessness had triumphed.

///

News from Poland. Yesterday I had a visit from a young man who has just come from Warsaw. There are leaflets and poems circulating in the country. They publish "black lists" with names of the collaborators. The punishment for resistance activities are long prison sentences, incidents of mysterious deaths have been mentioned. The movie houses are empty, theater attendance has dropped. I sat listening to a story about a priest who was forced one night into a car and driven blindfolded to the army barracks where he was made to hear the confessions of four soldiers sentenced to death for refusing to carry out an order. There's no telling if it's true or just a rumor. The public discussion between the opposition leaders locked up in the camps and the leaders, still active but in hiding, is amazing to observe. Kuron has sent from the camp a letter-manifesto addressed to the underground. Solidarity leadership, entitled: "You've Lost Your Golden Horn." A national debate concerning the means of action and the forms of resistance continues under the very noses of the army and the police. Texts are of extreme importance; the authors remain invisible. There seem to have emerged two different approaches; one favors negotiations with the authorities, the other calls for a general strike: negotiated compromise or bloodshed. My guest is for the shedding of blood. He says firmly, "Any other solution will risk slow emasculation." He claims there's only the illusion of a choice. There is no alternative, because the authorities don't want a compromise. My guest quotes in addition the opinion of his mother who lives in Wroclaw. "Thirty million would die? But six would remain, plus the seven abroad!"

The official press in Poland suddenly and coincidently published several articles on what should be done with the Polish Writers' Union, that suspended organization whose political image does not harmonize with martial law. The minority within that organization feels its power and goes on the offensive with the support of armored tanks and tear gas. The winners are the grinning idiot, the hero of the military television chats; the man with the small head, whose specialty is trips to Siberia and who is notorious for saying,

"Yes, Siberia is my hobby"; and the sugary hypocrite who steers the middle course between the Virgin Mary and the Red Star. Cartons full of their unread books are sitting in warehouses, like coffins in a mortuary.

Rule by mediocrity has been devastating. But in literature and art, the actual power has remained in the hands of those talented individuals on the side, pushed away, eliminated from the cadres. What could be worse than the torment of a committed, productive writer realizing that a handful of inept people has deprived him of the fruits of many years of work? It is their books that are being sold under the counter and translated into foreign languages. There have never been a hundred flowers. Always there have been just a few. And the revenge of vegetables is unavoidable.

In answering a French intellectual, who asked me at a social gathering at the home of my friends in Palaiseau whether I still felt any affinity with the left, I said, with an exceptional presence of mind, that at this point the left to me is simply a moral concept: The left are the people who will sit at the right hand of God. We stood together for a while, but somehow there was little left to say. No doubt he classified me under the heading, "The influence of Catholicism on the political neutralization of Polish intelligentsia."

My answer was sincere. What distinction exists for me today between the left and the right and in what sense such a distinction still lingers in my thinking, I described a year and a half ago in the second volume of my Diary. My notes said, in somewhat different words, the same thing I had said to the Frenchman at the party. But the intellectuals in the West are afraid to, or do not want to, or are unable to see the things that in Poland have already happened and to us are quite obvious. We know how it comes to pass that ideas of progress and justice turn into slogans of propaganda for new forms of oppression—how a socialist country builds prison camps guarded by police dogs for its workers. This Eastern-style egg of Columbus, having no right or left side, is called people's democracy, or real socialism. It was hatched by the culture of the lands of Eurasia, stamped with theocratic Islamic and Byzantine influences—a world with a different mentality and history than the West. "Was Khrushchev to the left or to the right of Stalin?", asks Kundera in one of his essays. One might as well ask whether Paul the First was to the right or to the left of Catherine the Great.

The opposition between left and right reflects the ethical and religious dichotomies of good and evil, heaven and hell, truth and lie. Totalitarianism blurs the distinctions, and eliminates the struggle between good and evil, because the evil is the good. Hell is paradise. A lie effectively performs the function of the truth. Minus signs are replaced by plus signs and vice versa. We must leave it to the dialecticians of the West to decipher what is on the right and what is on the left in this hugely overstaged theater of humanity.

The Poles, the Czechs, the Lithuanians no longer think in Europe's political categories. They abhor the perfidious means by which they have been deprived of the humanist decalogue. They have experienced the horror of an ascendant technology of nihilism—a horror that the West cannot comprehend. All the Parisian protests and revolutions seem not terribly serious in comparison with the political education of the Poles. They are asking me here whether I am on the left or on the right, while I wonder if God has not been bribed. And that is the end of our conversation. There's a deep void between us.

They say that in hell there isn't a right or a left side. This seems to be confirmed by the rather frequent mention of the circles of hell. In Italian churches I have seen medieval frescoes depicting hell. The souls of the condemned, intertwined in agony, do form a regular circle.

September–October,
New York

A month or so after we arrived in Paris, a formal invitation arrived from Columbia University, and I decided to accept it. We would be moving across the Atlantic for the third time in nine months. I had been recording a short weekly program for the *France Internationale* radio. Toward the end of August, before I left for New York, I spoke to my audience in Poland.

Today I must say goodbye and take leave of my listeners for an extended period of time. Beginning in September I shall be in the United States, in New York City. I have been invited by a school in New York, Columbia University, to become a writer-in-residence.

Writer in residence: In the United States, there is such a custom. A university will invite a writer and provide him with favorable working conditions, enabling him at the same time to be in contact with the students. I shall in addition give a series of lectures on contemporary Polish literature. But since it would be difficult to speak about contemporary literature without speaking about the literary works and traditions that have preceded and inspired it, I shall also be speaking about the past, or simply about Polish literature. And because you cannot speak about any literature without speaking about the country where it was produced, I shall speak about the country that is situated between Germany and Russia—about Poland.

//

The day after arriving in New York, I heard over the radio news about the August 31 events in Poland, in connection with the second anniversary of the Gdańsk Accords. There had been confrontations in fifty-three cities between the people and the militia, with four dead and many wounded. There were around five thousand arrests. People staged peaceful demonstrations; in the city of Lublin, the militia fired machine guns into a crowd of people, who laughed. Three days later, the press carried a news item about an action brought against four interned members of KOR (Workers' Defense Committee): Kuron, Michnik, Litynski, and Wujc. They had been charged with attempting to overthrow the country's political system by force. The statute provided for up to the death sentence. Indictments in absentia, based on the same statute, were issued against Lipski and Chojecki, who are temporarily living abroad. I know all six of them. We were in contact with each other in recent years when we all participated in protest activities, in publishing initiatives, and in *Zapis*. I saw Michnik and Chojecki more than the others. Our thinking went along similar lines; we had the same goals. We talked openly on many subjects, some of them political, which was all undoubtedly recorded. The officials who heard them know perfectly well what Kuron, Michnik, and the others talked about. They talked about everything but the overthrow by force of the system. But they nevertheless got the most severe verdicts possible. Indeed, they were despised precisely because they operated not by force but by intelligence. The police tend to tolerate intellectual or ethical theorizing; what they fear most and what they strike at is shrewd, intelligent action.

There is a phenomenon in Poland that can best be described with a poet's words: "The Poles, always talking long into the night." This, it seems to me, was the main substance of our lives. It sustained me during those years in Warsaw. We talked about Poland, about ourselves and others, at night and during the day, drunk and sober. There was an obsessiveness in the talk that suggested an addiction. None of us could do without it, and our need had a psychological source, like an interest in the occult. Returning home, I would often say, "Today it was good, today we linked the chain." The important thing was to establish an isolated, closed circuit.

With the help of words, we wanted to create a space of our own, a space in which we could be free. Our pronouncements on society, people, and books supplanted the injustice around us.

One winter, Adam Michnik came to see me, shivering in his summer jacket. He asked me what I thought was the source of ethics in a human being. I replied, his attitude toward himself. Michnik began to stutter. Tugging at a strand of hair over his ear, he muttered, "And I think it's his att . . . att . . . itude toward others." Perhaps we were speaking of the same thing: Your attitude toward others is a reflection of your attitude toward yourself, and vice versa.

After the declaration of the martial law, Michnik was placed at the Bialoleka camp, together with Kuron and others. Often I tried imagining what life was like for the interned, what the conversations were between them. And in the end I always concluded that a just Poland existed only in conversations. It existed nowhere else, and never would. A Polish ideal has been spoken, but not realized. Nevertheless, it has an effect.

The number killed—five. In Gdańsk they discovered the body of a young worker. It is supposed that the militia had clubbed him to death. I have been told of a slogan promoted by the ruling circles, "Ten thousand killed—ten years of calm."

October

I am now in my tenth month away from Poland, with no date set to return. The thought that I will perhaps never go back gives rise in me to a kind of psychological nausea. Once I had written in a letter from Berlin that for me it would be easier to endure two years of prison in Poland than to suffer the life of an exile. Saying "Poland," you usually have in mind certain landscapes, places, people, and a particular way of life. In this sense I am as accustomed to Poland as I am to my own skin or fingernails. After all, I'd lived there as many years as have elapsed between the Revolutions of 1848 and the First World War. But that is not the point. To me, Poland is the place where life is most authentic, taken most seriously, the only place where your own worth and soul can be truly tested. There I had grown used to a life of grave ambivalence: neither total freedom nor total slavery; neither total poverty nor total prosperity. With practice I had developed a sort of vitality stimulated by unsatisfied needs, sometimes fruitful. For years, much of what happened in Poland seemed to happen between extremes, in half-measure, or in make-believe; at certain periods, even communism appeared to be less than complete in Poland. And maybe the incompleteness was our true element. Maybe this is where "the dog is buried."

///

Last week, a certain Polish wife assaulted her American husband with the question, "Why is less and less being written in America about Poland? Why is it that, while that country is being destroyed in front of our very eyes, they're writing and talking only about Lebanon?"

The American husband thought for a moment. "Because your country is beyond help. We can still help Lebanon."

This dialogue took place in the evening, when American television, featuring a program on present-day life in Poland, showed a racing stable selling thoroughbred stallions.

///

The October air is warm and humid. We are living in a house on 119th Street, some three hundred steps from the university. Butler Hall, an early twentieth-century building, is fifteen stories high, has three elevators and four doormen in uniforms decorated with ornamental stripes. On the fifteenth floor there is a fashionable restaurant, the main lobby features a fountain, shaped like a swan with its beak lifted, and two palm trees. We live on the fourteenth floor. Our windows look out over Harlem and Central Park, and in the distance a group of skyscrapers, the far end of Fifth Avenue.

///

The presence of your native land in your system is constant, as if it were one of your senses, like the sense of hearing, or a dimension of your body, or a sharp pain, felt every minute of the day. Poland becomes increasingly internalized. From the outside come the news, information, letters that are layered over the images retained in the memory. A Poland from which you are absent is no longer a part of your experience, but merely a Poland related by others. Your life becomes a palimpsest of your own past, reports by others, facts and imagination. All this is confusing and painful, full of dark forebodings.

At a friend's dinner party in April, I had met a priest from Silesia, an ornithologist and bird breeder. He refused food, asking only for a glass of wine. The fifty-year-old man with graying hair and an angular head listened and observed us from behind his glasses, his gaze intelligent and intent. And then he began to speak.

My dear lady [addressing M.] in Poland you hear the cries of people who are being beaten. There is terror in Poland, my dear. Women ask us to give them words of encouragement, and we, the priests, are unable to find them. We cover up, we sit in silence behind the confessional. There is terrible hatred in Poland, ladies and gentlemen, the people hate the authorities, and the authorities hate the people. A seventeen-year-old boy gets a three years' prison sentence for hanging a red-and-white Polish flag, another's ribs are broken by the militia. The emperor is naked again, my dear Mrs. M. Now, how many times has that been the case? First after Stalin's death, then in December 1970, and finally in 1980, before August. The emperor has been shedding occasional pieces of clothing. But now he is naked to the bone, all that's left is a skeleton with a scythe. Our general has done that. Soldiers on Christmas leave with their families ran to their mothers and cried. But mother can't help. It is famine we fear, ladies and gentlemen, and pestilence, that they may attack the country, because in villages there were already outbreaks of mange and pediculosis. Only a miracle, the primate tells us, can save our society. But the priests can't work miracles, dear lady. All they can do is suffer together with the people. Inside the camps and the prisons, to be sure. Oh, the authorities are cunning: We're not going to arrest the priests, said one of the colonels, because that might ignite an explosion. The Russians don't want that, they'd rather go on sharing the world with America, so what can Poland do? Tanks guard the outskirts of the cities, and within the cities anger is rising. It is true that our neighbor sends us food supplies. But the stench of rotting fish from Russia pollutes the highways. And they say that professors from Kraków have asked to meet with the general. That he should give up that war of his and let us elect a president, like in Finland. But the general didn't let them near. That's our country, dear Mrs. M.

Saying this the priest seemed to smile with his bulging eyes. Then he turned to M. again. "In the prison camps, the women are the toughest." He took a sip of wine. "Here's to the ladies!"

I never saw the birdman-priest again. Yesterday, sitting on a park bench on Broadway, I remembered his monologue and how we all listened as if to a passage straight out of Polish literature. And it was then, as I sat next to two black men engaged in an argument, that it suddenly struck me that in the past ten months Poland has been gradually diminishing in my eyes as a reality, and was instead becoming literature. I keep trying to decipher it, to recall it. The thought that for the people in Poland the drama is an everyday struggle disturbs me and fills me with remorse.

///

Every few days, I travel by subway to various parts of the city, and every time I experience something of a shock. The feeling may be defined as a mixture of awe and fear. The word "terror" wouldn't reflect the feeling exactly, for it also contains an element of admiration, and even moments of rapture. Everything depends, of course, on my own mood; there are better and worse days. Milosz quotes Simone Weil: "I am suffering. It's better to say this than to say: this scenery is ugly." The ugliness of some of the streets of New York, however, is obvious, and objectively beyond question. Probably the city grew in a hurry, as cheaply as possible. The boxlike brick buildings had to accommodate a large number of tenants, and not until later was the Italian Renaissance and the baroque added on top or on the bottom. Here they stand today, ten stories high, gray, yellow, and brown, pasted with colorful posters, or else windowless, hollow inside, with boarded-up doors under a secession-style molding or an ornamental balustrade at the roof's edge. The city must have grown frantically, under the pressure of wild passions, and to this day has an aura of an infantile pursuit of happiness. An American utopia!

And yet, there is a kind of grandeur in this maniacal drive. You can sense the excitement of risk and drama, every bar and every small shop play for the highest stakes. Bankruptcy or riches, millions or poverty. Poverty? Among the ten million unemployed Americans, many second-generation families are living off government relief.

But then there are the temples of commerce. Once I was riding up on an escalator and watching a group of people seated on white chairs at white tables in a hall down below, while a long-haired violinist in a gold dress performed on the stage. There would have been nothing unusual in this except that I was looking at them way down there, while I kept moving higher and higher, passing one gallery of shops, bookstores, and restaurants after another. Here you can buy a cake, an umbrella, Gandhi's writings, a portable computer; you can see a film or have a pizza with iced tea. You approach the escalators through a graveled lobby with a pond and eucalyptus trees. Nothing new, really, only a different space composition. And somehow you can't help experiencing a sudden fascination. In this otherwise monstrous city, someone is always inventing new forms of a future life. This is impressive. Still, it makes you wonder! Are they happy or only pretending? How much of what they do is the result of courage, how much of fear or innocence? There's a great deal I find incomprehensible. I have no idea what their monuments are. Who is the general astride a horse at Fifth Avenue and the entrance to Central Park? In Berlin or Leningrad, I recognized the figures at once: This was Frederick and that was Peter. About America, I don't even have knowledge that comes from a sense of injustice: I know more about Germans or Russians. I am familiar with the depth of their evil.

Here I am amid the sins and the virtues of a passionate, greedy civilization. In no other city have I seen as many demented people. Or as many prophets, calling for a return to sanity. Here is humanity in the rough, with all of its ugliness, its crimes, triumphs, ideals, and illusions—this city oppresses and fascinates, but it does not lie. Here all the dreams and all the nightmares are out in the open; you can observe them with the naked eye, intersecting with each other.

//

Kent, in the state of Connecticut. Three sunny days, 120 kilometers out of New York City, in a one-story converted barn; three days in cool, clean air. The gently rolling hills, sloping toward the highway, are thickly covered with the rust, the purple, the gold, and the red of maples. It is quiet.

Down below is a lake, with a dock and a motel. You see no people walking along the roads, only passing cars. On the roads, alongside the hedges, stand wooden signs with names of the houses' owners. For the most part, these are one-story wooden houses, almost all of them white, with porches and mansards, with green, well-trimmed lawns in the front and the rear. "America is one-storied and white. I always said that, but they didn't want to believe it in Warsaw," says M. Yes, one-storied, clean painted. Light, happy, serene. The kind of houses I wanted to build when I was a child. The people living here are the people New York hadn't devoured. They'd managed to pluck a golden husk from the monster's hide and to exchange it for a little house with a green lawn. Now, once a week, they escape from the city to find an idyllic two-day interlude. Lines of parked cars surround the pinkish tennis court; men with pink faces hit their white balls back and forth; from the sky, at sunset, a pink glow settles on the white stripe along the black asphalt highway. Now and then the highway runs into a small square with a church, a post office, and a supermarket. Here again are the parked cars with children and dogs inside. Men in shirtsleeves and women dressed in jeans talk loudly as they load the groceries into the car trunks. Soon lights will go on inside the little houses.

All this has to be remembered. Along with the sociological data providing facts on the lives of the little houses' inhabitants, their depressions and alcoholism, the traumas of the "part-time widows." One must commit to memory the tennis courts, the children's laughter, the cocker spaniels in the cars, and the motel by the lake. The United States is one of the few ventures in human history that has proven to be successful.

//

Living in freedom is no paradise. The so-called free world guarantees man his freedom, but at the price of a constant strain on his energies. My own life in the West has, typically, compelled me to make continuous efforts, to intensify the will to live. The daily necessity to accomplish minor practical goals and the incessant preoccupation with this or that activity, turns your attention from matters of ultimate concern. There is little time here for worries about the absurdity of life, the passage of time, or about—pardon the expression—death. There is no time or place for worrying about your own end or the end of the world. In Poland, my feeling of impotence resulted in an existence of comparative ease and convenience. My goals were set low; I had no intense will to live. Compared to the strain freedom imposes, the lack of freedom may be a comfortable thing. There is so much spare time under socialism.

Unfreedom has its metaphysics and its nobility. I remember cold, empty evenings I spent lying under a blanket, in boredom and inertia, contemplating vague shadows moving along the ceiling. On one such evening, my doorbell rang. Lying there unshaven, I was not in the mood to open the door. I didn't drag myself out of bed until after the third ring. Janek

St., who had just arrived from Venezuela, walked in carrying flowers, took one look at me, and said, "Excuse me, but aren't you ill?" No, not at all, I was quite well. Like a slave, like a socialist prince.

///

The Gothic cathedrals say: next to God's majesty, you are no more than dust, fall on your knees before him in adoration and humility.

Protestant churches say: God is of your own dimension, respect him, be severe toward yourself, be thrifty, follow our example.

The synagogue says: God is within.

///

Yesterday, in the apartment of filmmaker Richard Adams on Fifty-eighth Street, I again had a dose of Poland "described." I was told about a report by a young woman from academic circles who had come from Warsaw a few days earlier on a three month scholarship. A report about beating and killing. During street protests, the police, in a fury, beat up not only the protesters but the onlookers as well. Nobody is safe. Gas grenades are tossed inside houses whenever a window curtain moves. A report about the arrested who can be bailed out for eighty thousand zlotys, but to raise such an amount has become increasingly difficult. About churches serving as centers of communication and meetings. Within the district, the church has become the clubhouse and the *salon*, for some it has taken the place of the café; it is where you see friends, find conversation. About generosity and sacrifice. Two elderly ladies hiding illegal leaflets in their garbage cans. Actress Maja Komorowska, who had spent the entire winter distributing packages to the interned in camps throughout the country. About the new attitudes of the intelligentsia. The editorial board of a certain monthly has held an hours' long meeting to consider the problems of the publication's future: If we're under an *occupation*, the monthly should not be published (collaboration with the enemy); if it's long-term *annexation*, the monthly has to be published (positive, "organic" work to improve the country). About a worker, twenty years old, shot by an agent of the secret police during a protest demonstration in Nowa Huta. They quoted someone saying, "This machine must be oiled with blood, otherwise it jams up."

At Nowa Huta, a crowd ten thousand strong fought all day with the armed police. They set fire to kiosks, dismantled railroad tracks. Lenin's statue was smeared with white paint while ZOMO men sprayed blue paint, marking individual demonstrators. All this was happening in a symbolic place, chosen thirty-five years ago as the bedrock of Polish socialism. Nowa Huta was built right next door to Kraków, so that the young working class could radiate its influence on the bastion of conservative reaction. And here it is, thirty-five years later . . .

Everything that the members of the government wear, from hats to underwear, as well as the cars they drive and the villas they live in, had been obtained through the efforts of the Polish worker, even the items imported from abroad. The government is unable to provide the working man of Poland with a pair of shoes for the winter. To balance this shortage in some way, the government imports from Japan such items as helmets, nightsticks, shields, and submachine guns. They are bought with money earned by Polish workers, and these shields, grenades, and helmets are being readied for the Polish workers. Social justice has been realized.

There are reports about cases of compulsory drafting of Solidarity members to ZOMO, primarily in the provinces. ZOMO—the equivalent of the SS in People's Poland—demonstrates a cruelty in their street confrontations with the population and a furious zeal bordering on bestiality. Newly released criminals are recruited for these state squads armed with Japanese equipment, confirming the hypothesis linking totalitarian systems with the criminal world. Stalin had allegedly used the services of Italian-American gangs, and Hitler's original fighting squads also included freed criminals in their ranks. Contemporary history teaches us that it is enough to have one mental patient, two idealists, and three hundred murderers to overpower, as well as muzzle, millions of people.

I am always astonished when I realize that M. and I, and our no longer so numerous contemporaries, have lived almost our entire lives witnessing this. Half a century! Christian prophets have long been predicting the coming of an Antichrist, but they never predicted there would be two, Hitler and Stalin, one right after the other, or almost simultaneously. You must be ever so careful when you are born.

Poles arriving from Poland say, "The war. Before the war." "Before the war" means before December 13, 1981. I heard this for the first time last winter, several weeks after arriving in New York. I was sitting in a coffee shop on Lexington Avenue with movie director Feliks Falk. Falk, the author of *Wodzirej* (The Dance Leader), didn't come to the States until after December 13, and was the one who used the expression several times. At first, I took it for a Warsaw joke, but when Falk repeated his "before the war" for the third or fourth time, I interrupted. "What war are you talking about, Feliks? Wasn't it a police operation?" Feliks appeared quite surprised. He described the currency of the expression in Poland. All right, I thought, they're exaggerating, evidently they need a heroic interpretation of events and so are promoting a coup staged by the army and the secret police to greater importance. Well, I was wrong. They were right. The term "war" was suggested to them by their acute sense of language and history. The intensity of the upheaval that took place on December 13, 1981, in the life of the individual as well as of the country—the collapse of existing reality, daily routine, and of values, the sudden end of a world—has historical antecedents in the Kościuszko uprising of 1794, the Polish-Russian war of 1830–31, and the Polish-German war of 1939.

Our third day at Stony Brook, fifty-five miles from New York City. Again one-story houses. Again green, trimmed lawns, two cars in front of every house, and no sign of people. We alone, the two of us, are treading down the shiny asphalt highway. October, the leaves have fallen, the autumn is melancholy, rustling. Daydreams.

Walking between the little houses, I try imagining how it would be to live American style. All you have to do is find the beat. And try to forget certain things. And fall into a rhythm of earning–buying–paying-off, and not remember "history." Americans have freed themselves from history; they've left it in the Old World. But no, I think to myself, this isn't for us. We can never learn the American ways; that other thing already has a hold on us, has stifled us. So we tread on, down the American road, between the little painted houses, with Plymouths and Buicks passing us at high speeds. The smiling passengers inside the cars, behind the windshields, are the people who had either inherited the little houses, or else had gotten them the hard way, who had pulled themselves up, leaving poverty and degradation in the backyards of their childhood. For them, it's especially easy to become American. People who are critical of the primitive ways of Americans should understand that the majority of their society has always consisted of the vigorous poor on their way up, climbing toward an ever-higher standard of living. This is their country.

What am I to do here without a profession or capital, with only my own background—the memory of four par-

titions, six million dead, several uprisings, a few Polish masterpieces, my language, my European, Mediterranean cultural
traditions, and the scars left from my own past errors? How
am I to repress all of this and become a smiling American?
And still only be an incomplete crippled American at that.

My condition as an exile in America gives me the illusion
of youthfulness. There is constant commotion—traveling,
telephone calls, correspondence, lectures, meetings. I get up
earlier than I ever have to be finished with my work by
eleven, to answer letters, send off paid bills at the post office
on Amsterdam Avenue, and walk down to the subway on
Broadway. Idling around is out of the question, my entire
day is tightly scheduled; only evenings afford me a few quiet
hours with a book and my own thoughts—exactly contrary
to my first stay in the United States, sixteen years ago, when
for three months I was taken on escorted tours of the country
by train and automobile. I had sailed on the Polish ship Batory
out of Gdynia, going to the America of my childhood, and
was confronted with the myth of an innocent world. The
book I was writing at the time was an attempt to discover
purity as symbolized perhaps by the sanctity of a cripple, or
the faithfulness of a dog. I imagined I would find confirmation
of my vision of a hospitable land in America, and wash away
my own shabbiness under the skies of the brave pioneers
who had twice crossed the Atlantic to come to the aid of
beleaguered Europe. I also hoped to find some trace of my
mother's prodigal brother, who, as a young boy, had been
sent by my grandfather to the United States, and later turned

up in Poland, before 1920, in a U.S. Army uniform, with a military mission of some kind, but soon returned to America, where he disappeared without a trace. (I later learned that Jan Landau had died a long time ago, allegedly in poverty.) What I in fact found was something totally different, not in the least what I had imagined. I found an America of vast, uninhabited landscapes and big, black-and-white cities, but the people, the human salt of the promised earth, appeared to me as a uniform *massa tabulattae,* living in the mechanized paradise of the petty bourgeois freed from his inferiority complex. I returned from this unfortunate expedition made older by a disappointment.

///

On my first night at Stony Brook I awoke after what seemed about ten minutes of dreaming and could not go back to sleep. I gave up trying and picked up a book from the night table: *The Magician of Lublin*, by Isaac Bashevis Singer, which transported me again into a dream, and what a dream! The streets of Warsaw! The main action takes place in nineteenth-century Warsaw, on the streets inhabited at that time by the Jews. I can remember them from before the war. Dark, noisy, lined with street vendors' stalls, with long courtyard passages resembling trading bazaars, where athletically built Jewish porters, with heavy ropes dangling over their shoulders, stood around in small groups. And store signs, a profusion of store signs. Platforms, piled up two stories high with giant rolls of wool and cotton fabrics, rattled through the streets as they rode over the rough pavement, while hairy-chested drivers with unbuttoned shirts shouted in hoarse voices, encouraging their horses to move along. But, in contrast to New York's Harlem, where a white pedestrian should never venture, I am told, these Jewish streets were safe, a person with a non-Jewish face could stroll over them quite safely. I couldn't reconstruct easily the new sections built in that spot after the war; I have always avoided them. On top of the heaps of rubble, they had put up rows of new apartment buildings. Were it possible to recover sounds from the past, and to hear come alive human voices from times and places that no longer exist, what cries of lament would resound throughout these apartment blocks.

The cries of the murdered people—I heard them one warm night in May. Two weeks had passed since my arrival in Paris when Krzysztof Pomian notified me he was organizing a public discussion on Polish-Jewish relations. I was invited as a participant. In a lecture hall across the street from the church of Saint-Germain-des-Prés, about two hundred people gathered about eight o'clock one night. We sat on a raised podium behind a long table: Paul Thibaud, the editor of Esprit, Pomian, Alexander Smolar, two representatives of the Jewish community in France (one was a member of the Chamber of Deputies, the other a young writer), and me. The people in the audience facing us were mostly from the older generation, with faces that all looked somehow familiar, although I couldn't say I had ever actually seen any of them before. Faces of Jews are always familiar looking; they seem to contain some common outline, probably a reflection of the Jewish faces one had seen before the war. Fifteen- to twenty-minute speeches followed one after the other, uninterrupted by discussion. The discussion was to take place during the second half of the meeting. One of the Frenchmen, a left-wing writer of Jewish origin, spoke just before me. He talked about anti-Semitism in prewar Poland. He cited facts. But somehow now, inside this stuffy auditorium, I had an almost physical certainty that these genuine facts added up to a generalized untruth. Poland persecuting the Jews; the Poles—a nation of Jew-haters. In the third row, an old man with a bald head and deep-set eyes without eyelashes was nodding in agreement, his palm curved around his ear. When it was time for me to speak, I felt tired even before I opened my mouth. To untangle the mass of mutual obsessions, to make up for centuries of prejudice, here in this crowded little auditorium . . . any rational argument would be useless. I spoke no more than a few minutes. I said that there wasn't, and never had been just *one* Poland. The same as there had never been just one France—there had been the France of Zola and the France of Maurras. There was the Poland of hatred and darkness, the Poland of xenophobia and intolerance, but at the same time there was a wise and enlightened Poland. I spoke of the Polish intelligentsia and its democratic traditions. I said that Poland was a nation that did not kill people. The Poles were not the ones who murdered the Polish Jews, although the Jews were indeed exterminated on Polish soil.

As I spoke, I kept expecting protests or interruptions from the audience. But no. They listened. I realized that this was exactly what they had wanted to hear, the words they had expected, and actually wished to be true. For a long time nobody interrupted me. It wasn't until almost the end of my talk that the bald old man rose from his chair and mumbled some words I couldn't understand at first. People tried silencing him, but he kept on, stuttering—he had a speech impediment as well. But I finally understood. He shouted that the Poles had betrayed their Jews. *"Trahi . . . ab . . . abandonné . . . !"*

The moderator intervened saying that the discussion would take place after the speeches, but several others then started speaking, and the confusion lasted for some time. After which came time for another speaker. It became very hot in the room; many of the men had taken off their coats. I paid little attention to the speeches that followed, now only hearing those other voices—the voices of the *betrayed* from Smocza and Pawia streets. Arguments? Go ahead, try finding arguments against heartache.

After seven hundred years of living on the same soil, the Poles have not shed a single tear over the Jews turned into ashes. Their surviving sons and brothers felt painfully offended precisely by the silence of the Poles after the holocaust. Not at the time of the extermination, but afterward. After the war. They had held no services in the small towns, offered no flowers. They moved into the vacant Jewish houses; grass grew over the graves in the cemeteries. The Church as well as the people were silent. They had decided to forget, to pretend the Jews never existed.

I had no courage to ask to speak again. I suspect that no one in the whole auditorium felt capable of uttering the words that were missing, the few most difficult and important words. I had neither the courage nor the certainty. Maybe there has been no mourning in Poland for the murdered Jews because new Jews have come in? Those who arrived with a foreign army, to rule and arrest? In the cemeteries there were still remnants of headstones, but flying through the streets of the small provincial towns were not the ghosts of the Jews, but rather rumors that the Russians had brought over new Jews, with changed names, dressed differently, in military caps: Jews who have removed the crown from the head of the white Polish eagle and ordered posters reading "Polish Home Army—the drooling dwarf of reaction" to be hung in town squares. And so perhaps fear and hatred had replaced compassion?

If this was the only reason why the memory of Israel, "the older brother," has not been revered in Polish towns, then at the Kremlin someone must surely have been grinning maliciously as he observed from a distance, with a satisfied smirk, the intended result of the move.

When the audience began dispersing around midnight, several people were still demanding to be heard. A thin man in an open shirt kept shouting that in some small town near Warsaw, the day after the Germans took over, the parish priest called for the people to burn down the synagogue, and the crowd obeyed the call.

With these shouts still echoing in my head, I left. I don't think everybody in that crowd had obeyed the call. I am convinced that people who don't want to kill and burn can be found in any crowd, and that God is on their side. Why one person will go along with the crowd to kill and burn, whereas another will go in the opposite direction, why this is so, I don't know.

The Poles . . . the Jews . . . today, anti-Semitism is almost always presented in the West as an issue between the Poles and the Jews, and is discussed—sometimes with scientific solemnity—with Polish examples. This is particularly offensive since in recent years there has been little mention of anti-semitism not only in Russia, the Ukraine, Austria, Romania, or France, but also in Germany. The Germans forty years ago were seized by a fit of genocide, but the Poles are the anti-Semites. Words often repeated are sometimes impossible to shake off. Journalists are capable of smothering every truth with words. And there finally comes a moment when you have nothing left to say. Thinking has been muddled by fools; it is too late for justice. It is better perhaps to leave the dead in peace.

Some traces will remain. Photographs, printed pages, remnants of graves, have survived. The number of people with personal recollections about Polish Jews will diminish. But the past will remain. I don't mean the time that is gone, I mean the world that has ceased to be. Dead worlds like this do not end;

eternity rests upon them. Three million people have lived in these towns, along with the Poles, and three million people went up in smoke. For seven hundred years, maybe more. Here they had said their prayers, lighted their candles, roasted their geese, and baked their breads, here they traded, produced children, and read books. For seven hundred years.

I suppose that—and I hope I am right—the annihilated world of the Polish Jew will in time acquire rare, enigmatic characteristics, and that in the future, the mysteries of his existence and destruction will cast a spell over the Polish imagination. Some still unborn poets will be writing verses about the former life of the now extinct star, and maybe some young person will again bend over the charred volume, fascinated.

This is what I expect. I don't know if expectations make any sense when everything has already happened.

///

Brezhnev is dead. I found two letters in the mail. The one from Warsaw was sent four weeks ago.

We try to escape the nothingness that is killing us. We are *déclassé*, ugly, we talk about shoes and food. Could Tomek use the shoes that you've left in your wardrobe? We find it hard to maintain our usual classy style, but we're still trying, as always. Today is Sunday. If you were coming to visit you'd get some really nifty homemade cake with nuts. And today Father Kolbe has been declared a saint.

These words were written by someone who had always managed to maintain style and class. Nifty homemade cake . . . there is desperation in that letter, I can tell. This then is how life is killed. Because it was once a life. You didn't like it too much, but still, it was a life. Occasionally it even seemed bright and full of meaning. I remember the mid-fifties, the time when the whole country suddenly resounded with debates, swarmed with new political and literary clubs and cabarets; a victorious generation, the young, filled the streets. Once I had been in bed with a bad case of flu, and after ten days at home I went out for the first time to see a performance, at the Hall of the Guards, of the theater of Villard that had just come from Paris. The large auditorium was filled with young people. I couldn't figure it out: What had happened? Everybody was dressed differently, wearing different hairstyles: girls with tiny waists, small heads with ponytails; boys in tight black trousers, bangs, wide-open shirts, dark glasses, white ruffles. When had they managed to change so much? Soon it became apparent that they talked and walked differently than we did, that they danced differently, and even had their own theaters. And later still I learned of a new nightclub, Largactil, the meeting place of a drinking, debating, music-making little crowd, made up of male and female students, philosophy professors, artists, and foreigners. Ah, this was really the good life. The young exuded a charm that fascinated and seduced foreigners who wrote about them in Western newspapers; here was life with flare, with spice. It was as though the price for socialism had already been paid, and now socialism was showing its human face, the smiling face of youth. The theater glittered with a full-scale international repertoire, television produced some very interesting plays, aired weekly; American, Swedish, and Italian films were featured in the movie houses. There seemed to be an increasing number of automobiles and restaurants. There were more passports issued, more neon lights. In the summer, students went to French vineyards to make money.

When the STS produced its program "The Smiling Face of Youth," the whole thing was probably over.

I do not remember the dates. I can't recall when I stopped walking from Krakowskie Przedmiescie and down Nowy Swiat to Czytelnik on Wiejska Street. I used to enjoy those walks. Along the "royal" itinerary I would meet many people I knew, well or less well, or people I didn't know but who knew me. I had a sense of being "at home." One day I noticed that the street had changed. I felt as if I'd been passing the same people over and over, people with the same impersonal look. Not one familiar face among them, nobody I'd even seen before. I don't know what year it was that the new social group had begun to predominate in the cities. Social change is not immediately noticeable, but the realization of it comes suddenly, in one day. That particular day, after walking down Nowy Swiat to Wiejska Street, I understood all at once that I was now living in a different city. The expression "peasant-bureaucrat" had come into vogue at that time. From a sociological viewpoint, the term was perhaps imprecise, but here were individuals of a specific psychophysical type. They were ever present in the streets, the shops, in restaurants, offices, at the universities. I consoled myself with an acknowledgment of the unavoidable price one must pay for any social transformation. But I no longer walked on Nowy Swiat.

And yet, life went on. People built houses, bought Fiat automobiles. Stores sold goods in fancy, shiny wrappers; and foreign films were still playing in movie houses. Modern office buildings and hotels shot up rapidly, new highways with overpasses cut across the center of the city. Young people no longer smiled carefree smiles, but the rational argument was still in force: This won't be a life of freedom, but it will be a *reality*.

They did everything possible not only to destroy life, but to distort it as well. While writing *A Question of Reality*, I left the house less and less often. As I've said before, I cannot remember dates. But I remember places. I told Tadeusz Konwicki, "Outside intervention won't be necessary. When things start to collapse, we will end up between their jaws, all on our own." He and I were standing at the stone gate of the Obory Palace.

Escape from nothingness . . . homemade cake with nuts . . . sometimes, for weeks or months, my life in Warsaw would be limited to writing, reading, and talking with friends. Once in a while I liked to take a walk in Lazienki Park or the Saski Garden. I also liked to drop in at the bookstore on Krakowskie Przedmiescie, ask about the latest publications. You could have a cup of coffee at the Telimena café, or buy a pair of shoes next door. On certain days, the city seemed very beautiful. Despite everything, life provided hope, a hope experienced in an almost physical sense, and generated by the presence of people, objects, and light. A hope accessible to everyone.

//

Sunday. Sitting in front of me is a thirty-year-old man dressed in a sweater, a scholar from Poland. We are talking about Poland, about Walesa and the general in dark glasses. He speaks slowly, in a muffled voice. When he hesitates, he tugs at his stubby dark beard.

Do you know he's a member of the gentry? With the coat of arms "Slepowron." Odd, isn't it? The rift is a very deep one; so much hatred between the ruling group and the people has probably never existed before. The young live hoping for revenge, and even if things changed for the better, there'd be no way to avoid retaliation. After what they've done to us, they will have to face the consequences. Such abuse can't be forgiven or forgotten; it's psychologically impossible. And don't think for a moment that on our side of the trench all is *caritas*. No . . . we've got our infernos as well. Mutual mistrust, insinuations. Jealousies. You must watch what you say, where, and to whom. And it's wise not to wear foreign-made shoes. A colleague said to me, "Why are you still hanging around? You've got your scholarship, get the hell out, leave room for others." That same colleague called someone an informer who had allegedly maintained that the key to getting out of the blind alley is economic reform. Careless. Such reasoning suggests you're a collaborator, classifies you as a renegade, or simply a rat. But then there are those who have converted to realism overnight. They watch each other's lips, hands. And shoes as well. You cannot breathe in that kind of atmosphere. Which is why I left . . .

///

The full force of the Polish language cannot be rendered in translation. How could a Frenchman or an American, receiving it translated, feel the same shiver down the spine as I felt when I heard, "You scoundrels, you wretches, ah, you scum, blast you!" The moment when these words were pronounced in 1968 on a Warsaw stage is still vivid in my memory, and I will never forget what happened to the audience. Finding a theatre piece in the classic repertoire affecting similarly a Paris or a London audience after one-and-a-half centuries, would not be easy. *The Robbers?* . . . *Hernani?* . . . not a chance. I can hear retorts: Because these are Polish themes that are now, finally, hitting the target with their political force, the unprintable analogy, thus awakening powerful emotion. I know many intelligent people who maintain that our celebration of our Polish literary masterpieces and laments over a lack of their appreciation abroad are unjustified, for it is indeed a literature with obviously nonuniversal characteristics, informed by the obsessions of a conquered land. To which I answer yes, it is indeed a literature with obsessions, but these are universal, the experiences and dreams of a conquered nation are universal, slavery is as universal a human condition as freedom.

///

The Russian spirit is unified by its submission to the state. The Polish spirit is split. In face of the most drastic and brutal manifestations of injustice, it experiences contempt and shame, hate and impotence simultaneously. For two hundred years the Poles have been in an impossible situation. They've preserved the memory of having been a great democratic nation, and feel a natural link with the modern civilized world, while at the same time being slaves brutally beaten by their overseers.

Some years ago, I wrote in the *Dzoker* (the *Joker*) about the West's blindness and ignorance of the phenomenon of national unfreedom, which the West has not experienced for a long time: It has become the subject matter for opera, the libretto for *Egmont* or *William Tell*. Truly contemporary literature—according to the West—centers its attention today on the unfreedom of the individual, with its social conditioning, its metaphysical limits of being and death. Lack of national independence? That is an affliction of backward countries.

///

In married life, different things will irritate a woman and a man. A woman is more apt to be annoyed by trivialities (M. complains I drink too many liquids). Men are disturbed by problems that are much more important. They hold their wives responsible, for example, for the fact that many Poles were killed in the Russian-Japanese war after being recruited into the Czarist armies.

December 1982

The weather is still beautiful. Dry, warm air, just like in Poland in September. I haven't written for a while; there have been bad days.

Gaja Kuron, Jacek's wife, was buried in a coffin draped with a sash on which the word Solidarity had been written. She had come out of the women's Goldapi camp for the interned with a lung disease. She died in a Lódź hospital where she had been in the care of Dr. Edelman, one of the surviving leaders of the ghetto uprising. Jacek Kuron was brought in from the prison to the bedside of his dying wife. He spent the last hours with her before her death. They allowed him to stay for the funeral, and I saw him standing next to the coffin, amid the crying and singing mourners. Four American TV channels have shown pictures taken inside the church and at the cemetery. Jacek, his cheeks hollow, his head uncovered, was dressed in a shirt opened at the neck and the same windbreaker he had worn when he came to Nowomiejska Street and to Obory. I didn't know his wife well. We had met only casually, the last time, I think, in the Old Town, in the fall, when she nodded with a smile as she passed me on the street while walking her dachshund, who resembled a small weasel. In the summer of 1977, the Woroszylskis gave a party on the occasion of Wiktor's fiftieth birthday. A tremendous number of people poured into their apartment. The only people not there were the recently arrested members of KOR. Today, as I think back on that birthday gathering, name by name, I can compile the list of people interned five years later. The house had been surrounded by secret agents, and when it started raining, someone came up with the idea to invite them upstairs, so they could warm up and get dry. Several people near me were talking about the arrested. "They say that Adam spends hours reading Proust. And what about Jacek . . . ?" "Jacek," said a slender, pretty woman, "Jacek is finally catching up on his sleep; he used to literally fall asleep on his feet!" It was Gaja Kuron. That was when I saw her for the first time, and I recall being somewhat taken aback. Kuron's wife? I had difficulty matching this lovely, delicate lady with Jacek's burly stamina, his weight. I used to call him a "husky bulldozer," and it never occurred to me he even had a wife. In time I discovered they were very much in love.

In yesterday's mail, somebody enclosed a copy of his letter mailed to a friend, but intended for me as well. It contained a description of Gaja Kuron's death.

She died on November 23, early in the morning. It was not cancer. The death certificate mentions fibrous disintegrating pneumonia, not properly healed in the past. She had only thirty percent of her lungs left, and asthma as well; she was suffocating. But she kept her serenity and was conscious to the end. They brought Jacek to Łódź to be at her side the day before she died (they had taken her to the hospital two days earlier, when her condition had worsened; before that she was with Dr. Edelman, in his own apartment). Jacek was with her for several hours. We have been told that they "played their roles" to the end, talking about her recovery. Gaja was under an oxygen tent. In the evening, Jacek was driven back to headquarters. Gaja remained fully conscious, joked about the nurse's catching cold if she stood by the open window. Gaja died in her sleep. As Dr. Edelman said, it was the easiest death possible for that type of illness (she could have choked to death). In the morning, Jacek was to have been brought to her side again. He hadn't slept, only dozed off in the early morning. They woke him up and led him to the service hall. He saw two officers and three glasses of tea. He said that right then and there he knew what had happened. The officers asked whether he wanted to see the body or to go back to Warsaw immediately.

. . . she had married Jacek when she was about eighteen, and when they took him the first time—for three years—she was left alone with the four-year-old Maciek. You know what happened later. As for me, I can't imagine our Warsaw world without her, or the world in general for that matter. And yet this is war, with warlike devastation. But I won't, I'm unable to, understand why there have to be casualties such as this one. And I am convinced that no one else's death could have had as much emotional impact as her death, and that it will compel us to do some serious thinking—about the future.

The American commentator's text followed the sequence of the TV shots with efficiency, explaining who the dead woman was, what her husband did, and why the funeral had not been attended by Walesa, whose name was mentioned in one of the songs the people were singing. Jacek Kuron was shown bending over the coffin with a choking spasm of pain (a close-up of his face), then Kuron at his wife's grave, clasping against his breast a young, crying person, and finally Kuron getting into an automobile and bidding his friends goodbye by briefly lifting his clasped hands. Then a cut to the relatively empty Saski garden, mothers with baby strollers, old people bundled up for warmth, feeding the swans with bits of bread. "The Poles," explained the commentator, "are tired by now, they don't want any more useless protests. The leadership of the outlawed Solidarity Union has called off the previously announced demonstrations. *No Strike in Poland.*" The announcer's face seemed to express genial satisfaction.

///

M.'s birthday falls on the last day of November; just so I would not forget it, a slip of paper with the date, ending in an exclamation mark, has sat for a week on top of my desk. And then I forgot. Tuesday morning I get up, hobble over to the shower, leaning on my umbrella as a walking stick (I've been having piercing nerve pains in my hip for the past several weeks), and, after ten minutes, return in my bathrobe. In the meantime, M. had awakened. I asked her how she slept. She smiled, not looking at me. I tell her about the sponge I've dropped and couldn't pick up. It is warm, a soft light floods in through the window shades. I wonder how long the Indian summer will last. "Unbelievable," I say, "just think, it's December . . ." M. has gotten up. I see her now with her back toward me, raising her arms to touch her hair, and it is this slow gesture that all at once revives my memory. We stand at the window with our arms around each other, then sit down on the bed. It is the last day of November; the sun is reflected in her hair and in her cameo ring. When at the corner of Foksal Street and Nowy Swiat I had wished her happy birthday for the first time, it had been a cold, humid day, and our combined age was barely over thirty. Today, it's over one hundred and thirty; the room is filled with sunshine, we have come a long way; many years have passed since that day, and no birthday wishes seem appropriate except the one, which neither of us dares to utter, because the thought that nature may refuse to grant it is even more terrifying than the thought of departing yourself.

At one o'clock I had to go to the Press Center on Fiftieth Street to tape an interview, together with Jakub Karpinski, for Venezuela. In the bus I sat down between two very fat black women with faces of kind nannies. They moved over a little to make room for me; I am wedged between them comfortably, leaning on my cane. The black women are large, warm, with sleepy, worried eyes. The ride takes about one hour; there are already traffic jams on Fifth Avenue. At the Press Center, I find the television crew waiting with their cables, reflectors, and camera. The Venezuelans are setting up the lights. Jakub Karpinski arrives five minutes later. A dark, mustachioed man sits between us. First, ten minutes with me, then ten with Karpinski. I begin to speak. The dark-haired man interrupts every three words to translate, shouting in Spanish to the camera. Suddenly there's a commotion. The Venezuelans apologize; they've run out of sound tape. Several of the crew members go out to buy a new cassette. They are gone a long time. The dark-haired man seems nervous. Karpinski and I try to calm him down by saying that similar mishaps occur in our own country as well. We wait, we look out the window. I telephone M., to say I'll be late, but she isn't at home; she has probably gone to the store. An hour later, the Venezuelans return in a sweat; they've found the cassette. So, again Jakub Karpinski and I sit down at the table with the mustachioed gent between us shouting away in Spanish. The end. The lights are turned off. I look at my watch: four-thirty. I telephone M., still no reply. She may have gone down to wait for me in the lobby; she doesn't like being alone in the apartment when I am late. I quickly put on my coat and say goodbye to the Venezuelans. Karpinski walks with me to the bus stop on Madison Avenue, the bus pulls up, I make a dash for it with my cane and climb in. Lost in my thoughts, I don't notice until after some time that all of the passengers in the bus, except me, are black. It's dark outside; there are only black people on the streets.

I have gotten on the wrong bus and landed in the very heart of Harlem. Men wearing hats sit on benches in front of the houses; wandering about are occasional groups of youths. The bus takes me farther and farther away from home. I get up and walk over to the driver. I ask him where I should get off, and I give him my address. Seated behind the driver is a young, skinny fellow. He shakes his head, clearly upset. "No, no, you better not get off here," and he suggests I return to my seat. "You in a big rush?" "My wife is waiting," I say, trying to turn it into a joke, but he is not smiling. "Don't get off now, I'll show you a stop where you can get a transfer. Still a long way . . ." I go back, sit down; we drive through empty, rubbish-littered squares. Wasn't this where they knifed Professor Friedman when he decided to visit Harlem? I feel strange. The bus is silent. The other passengers are not looking at me, but I know they are aware of my uneasiness. They appear to be looking straight ahead, but I am convinced that out of the corner of their eyes they see me, and are trying to avoid my presence. I am all alone in the midst of savage-looking faces, like a chicken in a lion's cage. Some of them are dozing. Swollen, protruding lips, flat nostrils, creased foreheads: The kindliness of the old nannies has vanished. Now they're a group, allied together, holding me at bay with their angry, hostile silence. Outside the windows, the night grows increasingly dark; occasional dim lights reveal the neglect and the ugliness of poverty. Human silhouettes move in the shadows of dilapidated front porches; drunken singing, howling, and mumbling emanate from the bars. Suddenly we are at a huge bridge, suspended in the darkness. There are no longer any streets: In front of us is an overpass packed with crawling cars, beneath which I can hear the rumbling of a train. I break out in a sweat. Looking around the bus, I don't meet a single glance. Just before the overpass, we swerve sharply to the left, the driver leans back, turning the wheel with all his might, steps on the gas, and the bus moves away from the bridge with a roar. Soon we can see lights and buildings, new passengers come aboard. The driver calls me over, pointing at something with his finger. I see a subway station. The bus stops. I get off, I run. I run with my cane, dash into the subway station, into the crowd, but suddenly there's the lion's cage again—no, a steel box, brown, noisy, crowded, with nothing but faces with shining teeth and eyeballs, and I among them, crushed from all sides.

For a long time I couldn't rid myself of the feeling that I had been in some terrible danger, that I had miraculously escaped from a perilous abyss, and that New York was a suffering monster, consumed from within by a mysterious evil, hidden and threatening.

I was afraid. But somehow not in a personal sense. That is, not for myself, for my own skin. I was frightened at the thought that the polluted streets of Harlem were a territory where humiliation must breed hatred and lust for revenge. I have stored in my memory a picture impossible to describe, the disgraceful ugliness of places that inspire fear, like the subterranean world of the rats; the dirty emptiness of the squares with skeletons of dead trees and the crust of trampled dirt (I had never before seen soil of this color, either in art or in nature), the half-ruined houses and the human shadows wandering in the dim lights, the eternal night of desolation.

The explanation that it was the blacks themselves who have brought Harlem to its ruin, and that the whites have fled the area long ago because of fear, is probably true, but does not change the reality. Reality does not reason; poverty and degradation look up from down under and observe with narrowed eyes the glittering towers of the richest city in the world.

//

I walk down Broadway, and I am surrounded with American ambiguities. You cannot determine anything unequivocally. A crowd dressed in loud colors, lacking the European sense of style. Empty, abandoned houses, the insane mumbling to themselves, the center of Manhattan filled to the point of bursting with riches, and all around the city a suburban

America of bucolic little houses. In this modern Babylon slowly consumed by all kinds of moral and physical cancers, you often encounter—more often in fact than any place else—evidence of consideration for the underprivileged. When New York's mayor condemned the crooks who used fake tokens to enter the subways and called them "social outcasts worse than lepers," the American Lepers' Association protested strongly. Mayor Koch apologized in public.

But, everything considered, if you're an individual who has failed, who is homeless and hungry, a starving artist, it is better to be in Paris than to be here. In America, even a man without a wife arouses his neighbors' suspicion and antagonism. The passengers on the Mayflower had brought with them their wives, their Bibles, and their axes to chop down trees. These three elements were to structure their lives, based upon strong will, efficiency, and virtue. Simple and beautiful.

Beautiful, yes, but have they skipped over something in their winning ardor, weakened the collective mental endurance, damaged some forces of balance that require long and patient cultivation? I am not sure.

//

Today, modern highways wind across the foothills of Oregon. Along the rocks, there are still deep grooves left by the ropes on which pioneers had lowered their horses and wagons to reach the fertile valleys to the west of the mountains. To settle these lands took an enormous effort. I think about this

as I observe the passengers in the subway car, riding downtown on the 1 train. Most of them are exhausted, virtually
no one talks, many of the passengers fall asleep during the
ride. You are struck by their often slipshod appearance, their
gloomy, suffering faces. This is New York's uptown crowd,
worn out by the city, barely conscious from fatigue. In the
subway you see the very lowest level of American society.
Looking at these people you begin to understand many things,
at first truly shocking. The criminal assaults on pedestrians
in midtown in broad daylight, the number of drug addicts
in the streets, the plague of cockroaches in New York apartments, the soup kitchens for the poor, the burned-out houses.
Such levels of degradation no longer exist in Western Europe.

The sights are bewildering. It is difficult to grasp the
general trend, the whole. Computers . . . cockroaches . . .
the Bible . . . homosexual weddings . . . a heart of aluminum
and plastic . . . the Statue of Liberty, with its torch . . . gas
chambers for criminals . . .

What am I writing about? For heaven's sake, tomorrow
is Christmas eve.

//

Tuesday. There are questions one is not especially eager to
answer. They may concern rather vague and complex
matters—or matters that seem quite obvious. L., who is well
informed on things American, wondered why I showed indifference toward the publication of fragments from *A Warsaw
Diary* in *The New York Times Magazine*. "It should be important

to you, the magazine has a huge circulation, it is read all over America." I found it really hard to explain why this fact did not excite me. Maybe it was because I don't particularly enjoy reading *The New York Times*, and have little fondness for the press in general, for the journalists and their world of suspect integrity that is supposed to keep us informed about the world. The world nowadays is terrible enough. I do not crave too much information about its horrors, especially in view of the fact that the information usually lacks objectivity and is often irresponsible. Thus, having your own name printed over a piece of text seems to a sane man to be not quite apropos, and certainly of short-lived value, a laughably meaningless episode in an avalanche of mutually obliterating events and wild acceleration of time, when tomorrow no one will remember what was written yesterday.

It may be that at a certain age you lose the capacity to experience true satisfaction. Especially when that age receives little social recognition, when respect for old age is not a value of universal culture. But what is culture? It's not a very precise concept. A person writes letters—that is culture. Another person collects family mementos—that is culture. Somebody prays on a grave, or teaches a child how to behave—that is culture. You are tempted to call it the "second sphere of life," the echo, the aura, the glow that must always accompany material and measurable aspects of life, so as to endow them with meaning. That second sphere of life requires careful treatment and patient cultivation, in many areas. Two people who spend an evening in conversation about the novels they have read, and who have beautifully bound books at home, exhibit their literary culture. The Renaissance granaries at the entrance to Kazimierz on the Vistula testify to the ancient agrarian culture of the region.

Quite frankly, I don't know how a culture of old age could exist in a world that does not respect its aged. To maintain its dignity and form, old age needs social recognition. Not reverence. Even if it's not now held in contempt, old age is surrounded almost everywhere by indifference. It is alone, alienated. The old are thus made older and more weary, their decrepitude and despair are increased. This is glaringly apparent in Poland, where youth is the only valued asset. But here too, every day I pass ghostlike creatures walking in the streets, such as the shriveled-up old lady pushed in a wheelchair by a large black woman; or the now familiar-looking couple: he, always in the lead, his dirty feet without socks, his shoes untied, his long neck bare, and his face bristling with white stubble; and she, treading behind him with a plastic shopping bag in her hand, dressed in an old, torn fur coat and much too large rubber boots, a pale smile glued to her face. Walking a few steps behind, she once noticed me turn around and look at him, and she nodded, almost cheerfully, with knowing acquiescence, as if to say, "So, what're *you* going to do . . ."

And am I supposed to rejoice that *The New York Times Magazine* has published my text? I tremble at the thought of the years that may still be ahead of me, years when I will no longer be able to tie my own shoelaces or have the strength to shave myself. Years of real, helpless old age, when you must hold on to people and to chairs. That is what I'm concerned with: dying, unnoticed by others, not *The New York Times Magazine*.

The old house, with a sagging mansard roof divided by three windows, and paint peeling around the corners, stood in the middle of a clearing. The clearing at one time must have been a part of the park, which after the war grew wild and became forest again. All that remained of the entrance gate were two moss-covered stone pillars. There must have once been a flower bed in front of the house, with a sundial in the middle, of which only the base was still standing, and around the flower bed, a wide driveway leading up to the now nonexistent front porch; the middle section of the front wall had been painted over. M. and I had gone there to visit my mother's sister, who spent two summer months each year in this country house. Several old ladies resided in rooms that were cool, permeated with sweet aromas, and furnished with weathered nineteenth-century furniture. I remember seeing black-and-white photographs in picture frames, decks of cards worn thin, and glazed earthenware washbasins and water pitchers in the bedrooms. Among the visitors, there were university professors, actors, wives of attorneys. At that time, we came together with a young film director and a good friend of his, a lady artist. We sat on folding garden chairs around a small table set for tea. From time to time one of the old ladies came out of the house, the hostess presented us, and we would bow to the elegant skeleton, whose withered hand rested on a cane. In the woods behind the house, our hostess told us, there were graves of insurgents of 1863, but it was difficult to recognize them; they have grown into and merged with those of the Russian soldiers of the First World War.

While we chatted, a silhouette of a woman dressed in white appeared in the back of the clearing, as though a delicate ghost was approaching us from the woods, with flowing, slow movements, the face transparent, a black band across the forehead. The woman came closer. White as chalk, a lifeless look in her eyes, she was carrying an immense bouquet of wild flowers on her arm. The loveliest of skeletons, I thought to myself. M. rose and went up to meet her. The woman looked at her steadily, I heard an exclamation, a sigh; a chalk-white arm went around M. and a husky, wonderfully melodious voice said, "I recognize you, but of course I do." They sat down together.

The conversation continued, about flowers and flower bouquets, about Odette and the cattleya episode, and later about mallows around Kraków. It was one of those conversations where the living blend with fictional characters and dead persons, with heroines of novels and the poets' muses. One of those conversations that literature couldn't do without, or possibly even exist without. They create a kind of second circle around literature, its voices resounding in unison: of repetitions, exclamations, gossip, and groans of admiration. And maybe these voices bring into being the final union between art and life, maybe they, in the end, are what makes art real for the people. But they must be natural. Only persons undamaged by art can talk in this way. Strange though it may sound, there are people to whom associating with art has done harm. It has imposed upon them obligations beyond their capabilities, caused them to lose simplicity, or even hide their good qualities for fear of being natural and thus appearing ordinary. In contact with art, such people fall under a mean spell and are overcome by confusion and fear. Unsure of their good taste, doubting their own eyes and ears, they take refuge in artificiality—a borrowed cult or a recommended contempt. They turn into insecure monsters, their faces always wearing a grimace either of adoration or cruelty.

The lady in white was smoking a Gauloise cigarette as she reclined next to M. in a wicker easy chair. Now and then she would utter a few words in a soft voice, distractedly, as if from behind some other thoughts. But every time she spoke, she impressed me by her unerring judgment and the dreamy intimacy with which she referred to poets dead for over a century. One could have thought she had known them personally. And I actually wondered for an instant where she came from. "Who was she?" I asked, as we got into the car. M. was astonished I hadn't guessed; she had spoken to me about her so often, about Madame W. . . . from Volhynia, who smoked French cigarettes in a long bamboo cigarette holder and subscribed to *La Revue des Deux Mondes,* and who was the love of Bunin, and Matisse before him, and also, it was said, some other well-known man. Cloistered in the small provincial town, hidden behind the double curtains that covered her windows, suffering from migraine whenever she returned from Paris or Geneva, the raven-haired Madame W. . . . with a velvet band across her forehead. Sometimes she was seen behind the grill of her garden fence, reading in the shade of a sun umbrella; books, gloves, and paintbrushes lay scattered on the grass around her easels.

The story I remember best is when M., as a little girl, was strolling with her mother along the main street of the small town and suddenly noticed at some distance Madame W. . . . walking with rapid steps down the middle of the main road, a black cape thrown over her shoulders and a black veil draped around her head. She leaned over M. and uncovered her face wet with tears. "He isn't here anymore, he's gone." It rained that day. Madame W. was rushing to the church, to pray for the soul of Stefan Zeromski.

//

I have intelligent listeners. Or rather, listeners with intelligent faces, because not one of them has spoken as yet. They don't say anything. It may well be that they feel as uneasy as I do, except that I must talk. The first lecture was attended by more than twenty students. Most of them young women, with discreetly smiling but very serious faces. Some of them take notes. The one who takes more notes than anybody else is a well-groomed, statuesque brunette with an artistic flair, possibly the wife of a doctor or an industrialist. The pale young woman with dark eyes seated on the right gives the impression of being a student interested mostly in sex. She is quite intriguing—she has set up a tape recorder. Over on the left, next to the door, sit two rather young boys. One has had a year studying agriculture in Poland, the other is a psychologist. The three happy-looking American girls, in white sneakers with denim purses hanging over their shoulders, don't speak Polish, but one is taking notes, so she must understand it. I asked the students to give me their names. The student sitting directly in front of me said, "I'm Marek."

///

After many years of living in Poland, interrupted by long visits abroad, I appreciate fully the pleasures of "being at home." After every trip, I would return as soon as possible to Warsaw—exhausted, and with great relief. An exile's lot, I felt, was full of anguish and untold suffering. Untold, because in my encounters with many exiles I noticed that they don't like to talk about their experience in exile, especially about the early, difficult stage. Here in America, I observe them at close range. A new exile must make a desperate, sometimes humiliating effort every single day to support himself, and only convulsive strokes keep him afloat and prevent him from sinking to the bottom. I have frequent contacts with people who are going through that first, that very worst phase. Young and old, of all professions. Students from Wroclaw sleeping in a stock room behind a shop, a friend of M.'s, a doctor from Łódź, who cleans offices on Wall Street ("at night I clean toilets for the Arabs, in the daytime I slave over my English . . ."). They come via Vienna, or straight from People's Poland—with the Poles' vision of a Californialike America, the land of plenty, where in a year's time a man will own his own house with a swimming pool and two cars. The letdown usually occurs about a month later. One day, in a dark subway tunnel, watching the shabbily dressed crowd packed together inside the dirty train, or running for the exits like a driven herd of cattle, the newcomer panics. Looking up at the magnificent skyscraper towers in the center of the city, he feels like a poor little mouse. He is frightened by the abandoned tenement houses inhabited by the homeless, and by the crowds milling through the streets. His feet are swollen from his many futile visits to the various offices and companies, his hand is numb from filling out forms and applications, his tongue is twisted from trying to pronounce English words, his brain is exhausted from the constant effort to understand slang. And he is seized by terror at the thought of what this city may do to him when all fails, when he no longer has anywhere to go.

There are those who cannot take it for more than a month; I've heard of attempted suicides. Many curse the hour they turned in their passports; some want to move on, to South Africa, to Australia. But new ones keep coming, from Warsaw, from Poznań, from Szczecin. Workers, scholars, engineers, former Solidarity members. They come with their wives and children, and they start from scratch.

///

This country is full of old women, Chinese, Jewish, Peruvian, very old women who speak little English. They live alone, or with their children and grandchildren, American high school and college graduates. Observing them in the shops, or in the city squares where they go to sit during the day, I am reminded of that most magnificent description of the pilgrims in exile in Stefan Zeromski's *Homeless People*. A new exile from Poland sitting on these park benches could hear many interesting tales indeed. These old, decrepit women know quite well how often in this great land you must feel death in your soul before you discover you have not perished yet. Because America will provide shelter, but not too easily, and not right away. It has always been so. The inhabitants of New York's Chinese, Polish, Italian, and Spanish neighborhoods, who march solemnly in their ethnic parades, are Americans today, but many of them were born in deepest poverty. The transformation from an immigrant to an American nearly always requires total sacrifice. For every person who becomes an American, another goes through purgatory. The courtyards of Columbia University are teeming with multiethnic crowds of students of various hues, loud, and rather sloppily dressed. Their relaxed, straightforward manner is enviable. As I walk across the campus, I often encounter faces with exceptionally clean, poetic features; I think I have never seen such romantic profiles as among American students. It may not be unreasonable to presume that many of them are the grandchildren of the old women from Podhale or Calabria who half a century earlier had experienced the horrors of the first years of exile.

Several days ago I watched a group of wretched refugees from Vietnam on television; loaded down with luggage in bundles, pushing carts with infants in front of them, they walked on a wet pavement toward an immigration center. There was a U.S. flag flapping in the wind, and I could tell that these people, having survived death and starvation in the camps, were now moving toward the American flag with uncertain steps, a little frightened. They were about to be accepted by America. Because America still accepts people.

"If it is a country that people don't want to run away from," Mr. Apfelbaum said to me last week, "if it is a country where you can talk with your clients about anything you want, and half of them have an old village somewhere in the world that they cherish, but want to live here, in this country—that means it's a good country."

///

Greenpoint is inhabited by Polish Americans who settled there long ago. Situated in the immense borough of Brooklyn, this is a small village with streets narrower and less congested than Broadway, and medium-sized, two-to-three-story buildings, mostly wooden, but on the outside imitating the "city" and plastered with advertising posters. The side streets are quiet, a little sad; apple trees grow in the backyards of the small houses. I am sometimes reminded of small provincial towns in Poland, for example Galicia or Zaglebie. Not beautiful, not ugly, but safe. Here there are little grocery stores selling sausages and dill pickles in large jars displayed in the windows. In the street, I hear Polish spoken every few steps. I was brought to this familiar-looking corner of the world in an old Ford, driven by two young men from the Pomost Club.

The clubroom was very much like a little café, with small tables and dimmed lights. The club's colorful president, a thirty-year-old man with a beard reaching down to his waist, greeted me at the door. The place was full, mostly with young people. I walked to the podium, sat down, and began reading a fragment of my *Diary* written in Paris.

I read for three quarters of an hour; you can generally sense an audience's reaction within a few minutes. Here, the reception was good, a sympathetic silence, now and then interrupted by laughter, always timely; once during the reading they started applauding. Afterward came the discussion, or actually a conversation; there were comments and questions. While answering the questions, I became aware that I was being closely watched by a man with a small moustache, dressed in a dark suit and a bow tie. He listened to my comments with interest, smiling knowingly. This one will most certainly speak up, I thought to myself. He's the type who will wait until the very end before coming out with some impressive titles or quotes, thus separating himself from the ordinary mortals.

He asked his question somewhat sooner than I expected,

right after somebody's comment about a well-known writer who spoke on Warsaw television in support of martial law. The audience seemed quite interested in the subject and the question asked by the man in the dark suit seemed to go unnoticed. So I didn't answer him until later, and only briefly, because other questions were already being asked. "It's not a pseudonym," I explained, "it simply is my name." Because what he had asked me I *did* hear quite clearly. He had stretched his neck in my direction and inquired with a polite smile, "Excuse my curiosity; perhaps it's indiscreet of me . . . but did you choose your pen name just . . . for fun? Does it have anything to do with the English 'brandy'? I'm very sorry to speak up like this . . . but I thought to myself, what an opportunity, so I thought I'd ask in person . . ." And he waited, gazing up at me with friendly curiosity.

I too examined his face briefly, smiling. Welcome, I thought, you tireless seeker of the sources, so we meet again, and, as in the past, again I read that question in your familiar eyes, "With whom do I have the honor?" No, it's not a pseudonym. It's my own, genuine "Askenazy" name, inherited from my parents and grandparents, though it may not sound particularly Jewish. But I won't tell you any more.

I could have said:

If you are really interested in the authenticity of my name, I shall gladly provide you with more detailed information. You may select from it whatever you find most applicable to my person. Near Prague, in Czechoslovakia, there is a town called Brandys.

In the seventeenth and eighteenth centuries, anti-Jewish persecutions took place in the town. The Jews of Brandys sought refuge in other countries: in Germany, Holland, Denmark, and later in North America. Some of them settled in Poland. The town's name assumed various endings as a family name. In Germany, they were usually named Brandis, in Denmark, Brandes (the critic and scholar Georg Brandes), in the United States there was a Supreme Court justice, Louis Brandeis, after whom a university has been named. In Poland, the original ending was kept in most cases. The Brandys families lived in southern and central Poland. Some of them had converted to Christianity in the eighteenth century, others held on to Judaism. In the beginning of the nineteenth century, there were Brandyses among the founders of Jewish manufacturing firms in Tomaszów Mazowiecki as well as landowners in the Kraków region. In 1863, one of the soldiers of the Polish January Uprising was Anna Brandys (her mother's family name was Wertheim). In the years 1890–1900, one of the Brandyses was a supplier for the Warsaw-Vienna railroad, another a high school teacher in Warsaw. Before the First World War, a young woman doctor of that name was an activist for Polish independence in the ranks of the Polish Socialist Party; her older brother became a professor at the Free University in Warsaw, after the war, and the younger one, a mathematician, taught at a Swiss university in Fribourg. During the war, a member of the Polish underground military organization and of Pilsudski's legions, Rudolf Brandys, was killed in one of the military encounters on the Eastern front, while a man named Henryk Brandys, owner of a Lódź bank between the wars, died in 1940 in a German prison at Pawiak during the German occupation. Some earlier information enriches, but also complicates, the picture. In 1794, a peasant named Tomasz Brandys provided Tadeusz Kościuszko with a raft to cross the Vistula river. It may therefore be supposed that some of the Christian converts of the

Brandys family had turned peasant, or that several centuries ago not only the Jewish population but the Czech population as well left the town of Brandys. Quite possibly this was the branch of the Brandys family that Reverend Jan Brandys, the chaplain of the Polish London emigrés, who died several years ago, came from. The genealogy became still more involved as a result of an item in the *Book of Nobility and Persons of Merit in Poland*, based on Niesiecki's *Book of Nobility*, and written by Hipolit Stupnicki. It reads: "Out of the crown extends an arm, slightly bent, holding a downturned sword, and in the helmet there is a similar such hand. The Brandys family once flourished in the land of Prussia, where Jan Giszkra Brandys was known as early as 1458." The description of the coat of arms, together with the above remarks, had been sent to me by a reader, a woman living in exile. It may be too much to presume that Benjamin Lewi Brandys, the miracle maker from Tarnów who lived three hundred and fifty years later, was the descendant of that Giszkra Brandys. But then . . . who knows? There have also been cases of conversions to Judaism.

And finally, I might also have added that the details of my origins have never interested me (which is not totally true), and that I don't classify people according to their ethnic origin or religious affiliation (which is true). Therefore it's hard for me fully to satisfy the curiosity aroused by my name. "The choice is yours," I would have concluded. "You may decide for yourself with whom you 'have the honor.' "

///

Some very young American women, seeing M. and myself talking with animation, sometimes loudly, as we walk along, stare at us with dumbfounded astonishment. We don't find it particularly upsetting, because we feel a certain pride in the more-than-half-century we have spent together, and also maybe a slight biological indifference toward the young; we too can appreciate the advantages of an age difference. And it amuses us to observe when suddenly there is a cool surprise in the eyes of the child of a friend of ours, who is writing his Ph.D. dissertation about a French writer, when he learns that the subject of his dissertation—a rather nice and affable man in person—had once reproached me for being too modest: "A writer cannot be modest, or it will be said that he is where he deserves to be."

It is sometimes said that people born after World War II are interested less in the authentic human being than in his specter, his duplicated, electronically transmitted reflection. The flesh-and-blood individual is now perceived as mediocre and lacking in definition. But what I myself still value most in man is his "self-formation," his ability to master his material being and to achieve a balance between contradictions from which he is never free. He must acquire the ability to express judgment, as well as to keep silent. What matters is not only what he says, but how he says it, as well as what he doesn't say. What intrigues me is how man is the product of relentless work on himself; how he cannot attain an integrated external form without adopting definite ideas or conceptions; how much in him is based on the material, how much on the ideal, and in what way those two natures permeate and shape one another.

I am reading *The Czech Wager* (Zaklad Czeski), and Milan Kundera's essay published in *Literary Notebooks* (a Polish literary periodical published in Paris). Kundera has come out with several volumes in prose, which have brought him international recognition. His *The Joke* and *The Book of Laughter and Forgetting* are truly outstanding works, and I consider his *Farewell Waltz* to be a masterpiece of the short novel genre. Furthermore, he grants interviews and writes essays. His works are of vital importance in the West, because the Czech writer has firmly confronted the Western intellectual with the presence of Central European culture, experience, and political wisdom, which may well contribute to the future of the West. Kundera says,

In the seventeenth and eighteenth centuries, the Czech nation found itself on the brink of annihilation. The Czechs know they could easily have consented to being totally absorbed by Germany, and if they exist today it is only because they have chosen to. . . . Their present existence is a choice, a task, or, to use Pascal's word, a *wager*. The nineteenth-century Czech intellectuals were wise enough to ask themselves the sensible question: Would it not perhaps be better, from the standpoint of the good of the people, to join in the already cultivated and refined great German culture rather than to waste the efforts in creating a new culture for a small country? Will Czech culture be able to find a distinctive character? Let us remember that about the time Czech literature was resurrected, Goethe had formulated his well-known conception that, "national literatures have lost their significance: the time has come for a universal literature." Czech literature had to join the world community, for only in such supranational space could it find protection and a guarantee of freedom.

Everything Kundera writes should be always read carefully, since it is written by a wise, free European, well aware of all that has happened and is still going on. *The Czech Wager* ought to be read with particular attention by every thinking Pole. Because in writing about the *Czech wager*, Kundera inadvertently reveals the uniqueness of the *Polish wager*. The Czech chooses "to be or not to be." The Pole chooses between manners of existence rather than between existence and annihilation.

///

All week long M. and I have been lying flat on our backs with the flu, side by side, all in white, like two statues on top of a sarcophagus. We were in good spirits. Outside, at the door, friends would leave us chicken soup. A beautiful black girl came to clean; under her short skirt I could see her black, corpulent thighs. As my temperature rose, I had sensations of euphoria. Music was playing on the radio, the sounds of some familiar minuet seemed to evoke visions, warm and explicit; voices heard one evening at JMR's came floating back; the time we sat in their kitchen with its painted plates lined along the wall, and Ewa, washing dishes, calling above the noise of the running water: "You must reread Balzac, I tell you, he's a great man, Wawrzek, go easy on that cake, do you remember what he said about the Slavs, or about artists? Fantastic, Wawrzek, up to bed, be sure and get *Cousin Pons*, it's full of treasures, Wawrzek, I'm warning you, and also *Cousine Bette*, you've no idea how much that man knew!" An apron tied over her full-length evening skirt, rubber gloves, her cheeks flushed, her face excited. The clatter of dishes drowned out by comments on French and Russian classics. The high-pitched, laughing voice, and the gesture with which she pushes back her hair from her forehead, using her forearm. The enchantment of that home-style mix of kitchen smells and literary masterpieces she sometimes did not finish reading so she could lend them to me as soon as possible. It is likely she didn't know how attractive I found her because of it. Now, resting in my bed, I try to figure out what Warsaw time is in relation to New York time; at this moment it's five o'clock, so they are asleep; I just heard three revolver shots on Morningside Drive, then silence, and now again music. The minuet, it seems, was Mozart's *Divertimento*.

Next morning, I lift my head from my sarcophagus and ask how much longer our crazy souls will wander through the rocky beyond, which, to me, does not so much resemble Elysium as some Aztec Hades . . . How much longer then?

My fever has subsided.

///

From notes for my lectures:

I have a great many complaints against modern literature, at least against a large portion of it. It has lost something that Conrad had estimated so highly: the rigor of existence. We know that the world is frightening, but nonetheless, since we want to live, somehow we must pull ourselves together and give a certain shape to our lives. Conrad had referred to this by using the French word *tenue*. I don't know if it is necessary, in our frightening world, to describe everything that torments us. Most likely we are awash in an absurd infinity. But consciousness and imagination diminish the chaos. The very description of reality makes it more encompassable. Someone is killed by chance, someone else, by chance, is saved. Someone is a scoundrel and prospers, someone else is honest and knows only defeat. What to do but describe it? In every good story justice is done. Conrad's formula of administering justice to the visible world is one of the most magnificent sentences ever written about literature.

Every community has its shared past. That past weighs heavily, always being present, and one cannot get rid of it. Russia's past, from the Byzantium and Mongol invasions, to the German-Czarist bureaucracy, weighs heavily upon the Russians and in a certain sense, defines their fate, functioning like ethnic genes. The Poles too have certain characteristics shaping their destiny, such as a memory of their splendid past and a natural sense of their ties to the civilized world. Poland is a nation that for three hundred years, from Kazimir the Great to the Swedish wars, had never been conquered by aggressors; during that same time, France was repeatedly threatened with partitions; civil and religious wars erupted throughout Europe: People found themselves in the role of humiliated slaves. Their feelings of contempt, impotence, and humiliation must have prompted their religious attitude toward history. Concrete historical details, which in Balzac or in the English novel have no supernatural meaning, in Polish literature acquire an irrational dimension and a metaphysical significance. They become providential. This may be the reason why Polish literature seems so difficult to classify in accordance with the historical-literary genealogies of Western literatures. One must remember this if one wants to speak about that literature intelligently.

April

How do I perceive the future, what do I expect? Sometimes I ask myself these questions and I think, you ought to have some kind of answer. Desires, nostalgia, intuition—they aren't enough, you must have an answer. One thing, I feel, is certain, namely that what Poland needs now is not an explosion, or bloodletting, or a return to the old, beaten path of collective sacrifice followed by nights of defeat, until a next holocaust; we have gone through this cycle of historical repetitions for the past two centuries and have already earned the admiration of the civilized world. Hence I am not in favor of any patriotic expectation *here*, of a heroic madness *there*. And I have no doubt whatsoever that there are other ways of saving national identity than two hundred thousand dead every forty years.

"The government has attacked the people and taken hostages." With this terrifying sentence, the author, who signed his name Maciej Poleski, began his article published in the Paris *Kultura* of December 13, 1981. It is clear that in Poland today the people's number-one enemy is the government, and to resist the government's destructive activity, you must first of all separate yourself from it. A zone must be created, impervious to contamination. Institutions must be government-run and so, alas, must be the schools and the theaters; actors must act and students go to class. But common sense tells us that in a Communist country, every move, every maneuver and slogan of the government and the party, is a fraud aimed at destroying the people. Politicians or writers who either delude themselves or pretend that it is possible to go into partnership or make deals with the government, are like contaminated fish—still afloat, yes, but belly up.

Informed members of society know all this, and as long as they know, all is not over. Forms of resistance, or even forms of existence, cannot be foreseen, since this requires time and the ability to learn from defeat. What can be saved after a defeat? Sixteen months of Solidarity and the principle of a self-governing republic—not long enough and too little to prepare a program for the next generation. Solidarity was a large organization torn by contradictions from within and exposed to provocations from without. No far-reaching political program could have emerged from that body. Toward the end, Solidarity no longer controlled its own movement and was losing its sense of reality; it had grown hoarse from debating. At the Solidarity meeting in Gdańsk, the members attempted to renounce their ties with KOR.

KOR had understood from the start that it was necessary at all costs to transcend the irreality of the system and to speak the language of truth. Thus, to seize the bill of rights from the government and show it to the workers: These are your rights. Before long, KOR had started the movement for free labor unions, which later gave birth to Solidarity. This was of decisive importance, for limited only to national and religious goals, it would not have achieved such a broad response or so much support throughout the world. Solidarity thus became an international symbol of struggle for political justice and the dignity of human work.

//

There are days when going back to Poland seems to me to be inevitable. Going back without illusions, with a heavy heart. I know in advance what I can expect. The taste of that poison is, indeed, more than familiar to me; I would merely have to swallow some more. And it wouldn't frighten me too much, since I would not be alone. I would return to share a common fate, in a week or so my absence would be nullified. It's happened before. But there are other days when the thought of returning seems cowardly and miserable, like an addiction. I can see the ceiling over my bed at dusk and the moving shadows, with their lurking, monotonous absurdity, easy, slumbering. I can feel that life sucking me in, the Poland experienced day by day, with its sacred as well as its ignoble elements. And this frightens me.

///

One of my acquaintances says, "Being a Pole is in itself a disaster. Being a Pole and a Jew is a disaster within a disaster. Being a Pole, a Jew, and a writer is triple disaster. Being a Pole, a Jew, a writer, and an exile is total disaster." "And being a Pole, a Jew, a writer, an exile, and a former Communist?" I ask. "That is Wat," my acquaintance replied.

Aleksander Wat had committed suicide in Paris. His illness lasted a long time; he suffered terrible pains in his head. In a letter written to his wife, he asked her forgiveness. He was an unforgettable man.

///

Wednesday. At eleven-thirty I am to have my right eye examined by an eye doctor. First a quick bath, and breakfast. At breakfast, I break my front tooth while biting on a roll. There's no time to shave. I telephone several friends; finally one at Columbia gives me the number of a dentist in Manhattan. I call him, the secretary takes down my name, but the dentist cannot see me until a week from now. I hurry to the bus stop, and at precisely eleven-thirty I appear at the eye doctor's office on Sixtieth Street. Dr. George Carter: slim, animated, bald, graying at the temples. He smiles, uncovering his large, white teeth. His movements are rapid, deft, staccato. On the wall hangs a photographed portrait of an old gentleman with a beard. Do I see flashes? No. I describe the web and the little fly. Odd, but that gentleman with the beard looks familiar. The doctor examines the bottom of my eye. Ultramodern equipment; I have never seen such instruments before. A fifteen-minute intermission, then the next examination. During the intermission I sit in the waiting room with two bejeweled American women hidden behind dark glasses; my eyes run with tears from the just-applied eye drops. The secretary fills out my application. The signature. I return to the doctor's office. "There's nothing serious," says Dr. Carter, smiling broadly. Relief. I can write. However, I should avoid sudden movements of the head, especially downward. Apparently it's not something that requires treatment; I must come again only if I see flashes. My glasses don't need changing, they are fine. As I listen, I keep glancing at the photograph of the gentleman with the beard, and I feel increasingly certain that I know him; yes, I can remember his voice. But from where? When? I write out a check to give to the secretary: fifty dollars, no cents. It's a ten-minute walk to the Polish Institute of Arts and Sciences. It's a sunny day, the skyscrapers reflect the sunlight; after the eye drops, the glare hurts my eyes, and at the same time the trees look blurred. M. is waiting for me at the institute. I get there unshaven and toothless. Quite a few people have already gathered, it's a social affair with wine and hors d'oeuvres. By now, the ladies know everything. They have done some telephoning and in an hour I will be received by a dentist, a Dr. Stewart on Third Avenue. I recount to M. my visit to Dr. Carter and tell her about the photograph of the gentleman with the beard. "It's a puzzle—I would swear I know him from Warsaw." "Not from Warsaw," says M., "but from Kraków. I forgot to tell you, it is his father, Professor Rosenhauch." No, she had not told me. Professor Rosenhauch, the famous eye surgeon, a Kraków celebrity; we had visited him one time just after the war. His older son Slawek, together with his fiancée, were killed in the Warsaw Uprising, but his younger son had survived. Slawek was Inge-Albertine's last great love. They were both hit by shell fragments as they carried the wounded into the Under the Eagles building. It's a small world—as one would say on such occasions. Not to me, however. To me, it has a tremendous range of possibilities. I take the Fifth Avenue bus downtown. The patriarchal beard of Professor Rosenhauch . . . shells bursting in front of the Under the Eagles building . . . the flower-strewn grave at Powazki cemetery . . . Professor Rosenhauch's beard flying across the ocean . . . Dr. Carter, Slawek's brother, examines my eye in New York. The world isn't small. At the corner of Forty-seventh Street I get off the bus and walk over to Third Avenue. Dr. Stewart's office is on the seventeenth floor. Mirrors, six elevators, doormen. I am greeted by a slim, dark-haired man in a white doctor's smock, with black brows, black eyes, and a moustache; his trousers are the color of doves. He bows with a low, welcoming gesture. Dr. Stewart looks like an Italian tenor, has a melodious, clear voice, flowing movements, and sensitive eyes. "We can match it on the spot, glue it together, ha ha ha ha!" On the walls are hanging his diplomas, Prince Pepi and Kościuszko, dressed in a peasant russet, seated on a horse, and with a dog. Farther down there is a little shelf, and on the little shelf stands a bust of Chopin. Soft recorded music, and a view above the skyscrapers. Next to the dentist's chair, a white instrument with laughing gas, ha ha ha. In his pleasant, soft tenor, Dr. Stewart tells me how he came from Lublin to the United States. Actually, he followed the woman he loved. I examine the photographs of his two small daughters, and within an hour I have a new tooth. "Please accept it as a gift," a maestro's bow, his arm on his chest, "and please, don't say any more, it's entirely my pleasure!" "But, dear doctor . . ." "Ha ha ha!" sang out Dr. Stewart, "best wishes to you!" I put my arms around him. I ride up on Madison Avenue bus number M-4; the fog has lifted, the sidewalks are filled with a lively crowd. A beautiful day, warm and full of color; people are walking around with their coats unbuttoned. A truly beautiful day.

//

Inside my mailbox, a newspaper and three letters. Two from France, the third in an envelope with Polish stamps. On my way to the elevator, I glance at the sender's address. I stop: *Adam Michnik, Warsaw, Rakowiecka 37 "M"*.

Dated February 18: When you receive this letter, it will probably be after the final verdict. The hearings are just about over. I feel fine, mentally in particular. It's a huge luxury for so many months not to sin, not to waste time, to be able to straighten out your thoughts and to come to peace with yourself. I haven't been in such a fine mental state for years. The conditions here are pretty bad, but you can get to like almost anything. The food is scarce and lousy, but then I am able to maintain my slim figure. They've got a good library, so I am studying Bunin and Mann, and I am brushing up on my French every day. I shall try to get permission in this penal institution to write my doctoral dissertation.

He was wrong. Not only had they not reached a verdict, but the trial itself hadn't even begun. They had probably decided that it should take place after the Pope's visit. Or . . . ? The Pope is to arrive in June. The price of this visit is not yet known publicly. If, however, on the day of Pope John Paul's arrival an amnesty for political prisoners in Poland were to be announced, then it would be known. But if the trial takes place later, if the verdicts are announced in Warsaw after the Pope departs for Rome, then the price that the Holy Father had agreed to pay to come to Poland and the conditions set by the government will still be unknown. I am afraid that of the numerous unsolved mysteries of this world, this is one more we may never penetrate. Michnik on Rakowiecka Street is bound to have similar thoughts, otherwise how should I interpret his remark about the doctoral dissertation inside a penal institution (which is to say, after the verdict).

Letters written by the political prisoners are censored more severely than others. Someone had brought from Warsaw one such letter, made illegible, with entire paragraphs crossed out. Michnik's letter, on the other hand, arrived untouched, and had it not been for the envelope with the sender's prison address, Polish stamps and postmark, one could have thought it arrived through private channels.

Not even one deletion. I am guessing that the prison censors decided, on reflection, to send Michnik's letter to higher authorities, who then let it pass unchanged, without deletions. Possibly it was considered a good item to export to the West, good publicity for the liberalism of the post-December government in Poland. What a tolerant administration! It allows a prisoner to conclude a letter with these words:

The worst thing is that we have such miserable lighting, and there isn't a ghost of a chance of getting another bulb, because— as I've been informed—"then everybody would want one, and a prison has its limits." (sic!!!). In addition, the toilet isn't separated by a partition, which for those of us with decadent bourgeois upbringing can be rather uncomfortable. However, getting a permit for a partition is as easy as capturing the Bastille, and the Bastille still stands firm. But—as comrade Stalin used to say—there are no fortresses that the Bolsheviks are unable to conquer.

Michnik is in prison for the third time, not counting the numerous forty-eight-hour arrests. In 1968 they kept him locked up for two years; he was then twenty-two years old. In 1977 he was in for several weeks; along with other members of KOR he was released after the proclamation of an amnesty. He didn't like to talk about these events. When I asked him if he found prison difficult to take, he merely remarked that he was badly treated because he refused to testify during interrogations. "It just isn't fit for human beings," he shrugged his shoulders, "and on top of it, I like girls a lot . . ." I remember that he said it without smiling, not at all as a joke, and that my question was probably unpleasant to him.

M. is convinced there will never be a trial, because Adam, Jacek Kuron, and the rest will certainly be included in the amnesty. She warms up to that idea, produces arguments. Her eyes shine: "What do you say? Let's make a bet!" No. Besides, I don't know what we could bet with. And I don't even know to what extent she believes it herself. Her arguments are often persuasive. While speaking against fate, M. brings to bear all the dazzling resources of her eloquence, and at such moments she is formidable. I never try penetrating the innermost recesses of her heart, so that when she has already convinced me and the others, I don't ask whether she has also convinced herself. It seems better that way, even though her predictions don't always come true. But then we don't talk about it. New issues come up that M. solemnly attacks with her voice, her look, her gestures, tireless in her role of the good prophet. At first I listen with astonishment, then I want to interrupt. But at the same time it occurs to me that you mustn't interfere with the efforts of those who are trying to influence favorably the course of the stars.

Another trip to Paris. At the consulate, I have taken care of the visas. I have sent a letter to the Cité des Arts asking them to reserve an *atelier* for the month of June. In the meantime, we shall have to come up with some furniture if we want to live on François-Miron Street. Our future living quarters are to be renovated, but are now empty. It is usually said in such situations that "people will help." But what if they don't? I see myself carrying a heavy wardrobe up the boulevards in the heat of the day. A table. A bed. A couple of chairs. An armchair to write in. A lamp. I add it all in French francs, end up with a frightening sum, and lie there, contemplating my Paris budget. What modest sources of income indeed: fees from *Gallimard* for the French edition of my *Diary* and *Radio France Internationale* for my weekly essay. And then, only the lectures at the *Ecole des Hautes Etudes*, mentioned in Milan Kundera's letter. A difficult decision. And, in addition, all the figures could collapse as a result of one illness: for M.'s ambulance and examination at New York Hospital, I received a bill for five hundred dollars.

Soon it will be time to say goodbye and pack our suitcases. The winter things will go by sea; we shall travel by air. Our fourth ocean crossing in a year and a half. Yesterday, as I rode in a taxi across the Triboro Bridge, I turned around and saw an unfamiliar view of Manhattan through the rear window. Under low-lying clouds. A bluish-black, sagging sky, and Manhattan, as if suspended from the clouds. Yellow-and-green smoke from the chemical plants lingered in the foreground, and behind it I saw clouds hanging over the high, silvery "Twin Towers," and the building with the slanted roof resembling a sail. A helicopter circled around the pinnacle of the Empire State Building. The sight was fantastic, almost requiring background music. I am aware that I may be saying goodbye to New York for a long time, possibly forever. And I leave it with mixed emotions. Nowhere else have I been so free politically, or so exhausted physically. No other city in the world has inspired in me so much awe and admiration, and no other city has made me feel as much a stranger. An amazing city. Its ugliness is pathetic, its beauty astounding.

May

A poor harvest from my last month in New York. All I have to show for it are a few loose pages and some notes:

I spend the first of May listening to the radio and watching TV. On the television news there are reports of demonstrations in Gdańsk and Warsaw. The fury of the ZOMO forces, their relentless zeal, cruelty, and the protestors' desperate resistance were quite evident. Terrifying scenes. Women thrown to the ground and dragged away. A man holding his head after being struck with a club. A battered boy being carried from the crowd. ZOMO men, in helmets and gas masks, with their armor coats and long, white clubs, looking like creatures from another planet. There have been demonstrations in many cities. Poland—the only country in the

Communist bloc where on May 1 the police beat up the population protesting in the streets.

Tuesday, May 3. The last day of the academic year, a farewell meeting with my auditors in the lecture hall on the fifteenth floor. A warm, friendly atmosphere, a table decorated with little red-and-white flags and a flower vase full of carnations, also red and white. They've presented me with a watch and a thank you letter on a piece of cardboard in the shape of the Brooklyn Bridge. I couldn't bring myself to speak to them as a deeply moved professor, and I simply proposed a toast to their good health. Posing together for commemorative photographs. One of the coeds (the mysterious one who had so diligently taped all my lectures) got drunk. Out of the window we could see the college yard and picnicking students. They had spread out tablecloths on the grass; we could hear the strumming of a guitar. They sang and danced.

Many things to do and people to see before leaving; there's little time for regular writing. May 9, the anniversary of the end of the war—there are no articles in the press about it, no gun salutes. They obviously forgot the anniversary of their own victory. The Vietnam defeat left more of an impression; this they did not forget.

June

I left New York on the fourth with four suitcases, a type-writer, a bag, a carry-on case, and two umbrellas. I put my diary in the bag. Once inside the plane, I felt relieved: seven hours, a whole night of flying. Not until morning would I have to struggle with the luggage at Orly airport, and find a taxi, after weeks of trying to acquire and transport furniture, plus handling the various formalities. I decided not to think about it for a while. After an hour over the ocean I felt quite relaxed and walked to the washroom to rinse my face. When the incredible announcement came from the pilot's cabin, I wasn't certain I quite understood what it meant.

We had been flying over the Atlantic for an hour and a

half inside a Transamerican Airlines plane that had taken off from Kennedy Airport at 8 P.M. United States time. The 350 passengers had begun to settle down for the night. Some had already dozed off; others were smoking and reading their newspapers. Some were drinking fruit juices, some were adjusting their air-control knobs. The plane was filled to capacity. In back of me sat a jolly Frenchman from Marseilles who never stopped talking. In front of me, a pretty young woman, her hair thrown over the back of her seat, was leafing through a picture magazine, chewing gum. Next to me sat a quiet man with a dark beard, engrossed in a detective novel. Across the aisle was seated an extremely tall, intellectual-looking American, while his young wife and their seven-year-old boy sat several seats away; every few minutes there were family visits; the boy would come over with his book and ask that it be read aloud. The stewardesses began serving trays with food. There was no turbulence. People started turning off their little lamps and wrapping themselves in blankets. This was when I had decided to go to the washroom, only to hear a few seconds later, just as I was drying my hands, the pilot's voice: "Ladies and gentlemen, we're re-turning to JFK Airport in New York."

When I got back to my seat, I saw no signs of panic. It didn't seem as though anything out of the ordinary had happened, except that the man from Marseilles was now silent and the redhead in front had tied her hair in a bun. My bearded neighbor continued to read his story, though his fingers seemed to have tightened around the book; his fingernails looked quite white. M. and I talked, pretending we didn't notice the tall American ask his neighbors if they wouldn't mind changing places with his wife and son. From then on the family sat together, the wife holding her husband's hand, the boy looking at pictures in a book (I noticed the title: *More Money*). The pilot did not say anything more. I stopped a passing flight attendant. They had discovered an oil leak in one of the engines.

We were flying through a misty glow, high above the clouds. Nobody talked. M. tugged at my hand. "We're over land." I must have dozed off, because I hadn't heard the second announcement from the captain's cabin. We were now flying over the state of Massachusetts; another plane was already waiting for us in New York. The moment our wheels touched the asphalt runway at Kennedy Airport, there was a sigh of relief and people started applauding. After a two-hour wait, we took off again with the same crew in an identical white-and-green Transamerican Airlines plane. The flight was uneventful. I rolled myself up in a blanket, and was awakened by bright, harsh daylight. It was noon. We had begun our descent over France. At Orly Airport, the crew bid us farewell at the exit. The pilot, a middle-aged man with a ruddy face and light-colored eyebrows, laughed and patted my shoulder when I said thank you.

M. and I ran with my traveling bag, my typewriter, and my umbrella through a large crowd of passengers who ten hours earlier might have fallen into the ocean in their life jackets, and, frantically pushing and shoving, we threw ourselves at the luggage carts. I lost the bag with my manuscript, but M. recovered it at the taxi stand. We rode in a taxi along the Seine and caught a glimpse of the winged statue on Châtelet. I was unshaved, my feet were swollen, I wondered where I'd get the furniture for our new apartment and decided I'd probably have to go back to Warsaw. Two days later we were standing inside our empty, white apartment with its bare walls and creaking floors, looking around and saying it had pretty good light, and wondering how many years we would live there.

It all seemed strange. M. and I walked through the clean, white rooms where we were about to start life all over again. M. wore a light blouse, her hair was fluffy, freshly washed; she said, "I promise you it will work, somehow." I felt a deep shiver, such as one may feel when dreaming that one is standing on top of a ladder with nothing to lean against. But later that day we went to Saint-Paul and I saw M. walking among the fruit-filled stalls of the market, chatting with a fat stall owner while picking out fruit, touching it with her fingers. I felt fine.

///

During the days of the Pope's visit, Poland has again become front-page news. It is again prominent in the press and on TV, with its former, even traditional presence, making the French a bit uneasy. "To the West," I was told by a very intelligent Frenchman, "Poland has been for two hundred years nothing more than a quiver of conscience." He reminded me that

Chopin, in his letters to his family, described the allegorical spectacles shown in Paris theatres after the collapse of Poland's November Insurrection. They pictured the glory and the martyrdom of the heroic Poles; on the stage, red-and-white flags fluttered in the air to the thunder of artillery fire; the audience cheered. In the nineteenth century, France was flooded with pamphlets, articles, and proclamations in support of the Polish cause. Poland had become the symbol of suppressed liberty; it disturbed people's consciences. But as a political, economic entity, as a distinctive culture, it had ceased to exist for the West long before. They wrote and spoke of Poland as the martyred spirit floating over the Europe of emperors. They wrote about it with compassion and not without a sense of guilt. At least, that's how it was until the Paris Commune. Many Poles had fought on the side of the Communards, some even became generals of the Commune. After the suppression of the insurrection, the French bourgeoisie, still terrified, turned their fears against the Poles. Tens of thousands of Poles were put before the firing squads. It was no longer said *les braves Polonais*. And finally, in 1939, came the disdainful, rhetorical *mourir pour Danzig?* . . . with a big question mark. It was easy to justify one's behavior toward a defeated nation that proved to be unequal to its task.

And what about now?

//

When, after December 13, a new wave of Polish exiles poured into the West, they were offered living accommodations and jobs. Now, three years later, there is still much sympathy for the Poles; rallies proclaiming solidarity with Poland are still being organized (I was recently at one such gathering at the huge Mutualité hall, where several thousand people chanted the names of Walesa and Kuron), but at the same time I am being asked more and more often about Polish anti-Semitism. It has come in with the wave of the exiles, it is here, and it is beginning to leave its mark. Polish anti-Semitism—verbose and flippant. Not bloodthirsty or cruel, just thoughtless. Occasionally, it is brought in by young people who have never even seen a Jew, but who speak about the Jews with disgust. In Canada, a Polish-language periodical has just appeared with the emblem of Solidarity in its title and threats against the American Jews on its front page. The excellent Polish daily in New York, *Nowy Dziennik*, received abusive letters after it printed a series of articles commemorating the uprising in the Warsaw Ghetto. In Paris, three days after my arrival, I heard a twenty-eight-year-old exile from Toruń say that if a Pole wants to obtain an apartment grant, he must first give a bottle of vodka to the Jew at the mayoralty. She hadn't seen a Jew in Toruń, or at the mayoralty. She was not an evil person, but she had been told that the Jews were evil. Polish anti-Semitism today pronounces the word *Jew* as though it were a sound referring to the mean powers of fate. The word *Jew* does not denote a concrete, flesh-and-blood person, but an impersonal, malicious power that has to be given a name. Evidently, nothing has gone to waste. Neither the old, clerical and nationalistic anti-Semitism, nor the new, Communist anti-Semitism, coming from the East.

//

A certain honest man fell upon me with accusations during a get-together at Wiktor Woroszylski's home in Zoliborz. My *Warsaw Diary* had just come out. He came to sit next to me and burst out, "Why're you harping on the same subject again? Jews, anti-Semitism . . . do you really have to write about it all the time? It's gotten to be an obsession with you." He was a friend and I could not suspect him of anti-Jewish discrimination. I was anxious to explain to him why I went on writing *on that subject*. I spoke about the metaphysical dimension of the crime committed against the Jews. I said that one can never stop thinking about the annihilation of the Jews—it will remain forever in human memory, like the books of the Bible, and, having been witness to it, I would write about it for the rest of my life. I spoke of the six million dead. I asked him whether he understood what I was saying. It seemed to me that he didn't want to understand. He had had a few drinks, anyway, and he probably regretted the following day that he had brought up the subject. Here was a decent, intelligent Pole, a man of integrity; one of the many decent people, however, who don't like talking about the Jewish holocaust. Some issues have always been passed over in silence in Poland; it is an old and deep-rooted tradition.

Here is another reason why I keep returning to this subject. Because the anti-Semites aren't silent. They go on spewing the same old rubbish. Anti-Semitism has always been stupid and loathsome. At one time, there was an attempt to approach it as a social problem, to analyze its causes—study it intellectually. Today, it's nothing but a demon that gets into some people. No rational argument can deal with it; it belongs to the family of the small, vulgar devils who won't go away until they are properly exorcised.

//

The apartment on François-Miron Street. A long hallway, white and narrow. Where it ends there's a bathroom, well equipped, with a window and wall cabinet. To the right, off the hall, a large kitchen, also with a window and wall cabinets. Farther down along that side, M.'s room, sunny, with a half-balcony (and the wardrobe from Mira T.) To the left, three unconnected rooms. I work and sleep in one, two are not yet furnished. All three have windows that look out onto the street; they're not sunny, but very bright. The house was built in the 1930s and has an elevator. You enter the house after pressing four buttons, in accordance with a code. The *concierge* is a young Portuguese woman with a husband, Mr. Drago. The apartment is under city management, with rents about half the price of similar apartments in the neighborhood. François-Miron Street runs in a semicircle from the St. Gervais Church to the Rivoli and Saint-Paul. To the north, it borders on the old streets of Le Marais, to the southwest there is the Seine, with the Louis-Philippe bridge leading to the island. Saint Gervais had a brother, Saint Protais. I have been assured that Mickiewicz, having visited these parts quite often, must have seen the church numerous times. To the west is the Bastille, to the south, the Panthéon.

This is where I eat and sleep. This is where I live. Paris is a beautiful city ("is it really so beautiful, now that I am here?" asked Wilek Mach). It is also a beautiful city because I know it. It is the same as with books. The most beautiful books are those that you read over and over, those that you know by heart, or else those read to you a long time ago.

My familiarity with Paris is far from reciprocal. I know it better than it knows me. There is reciprocity in my familiarity with Warsaw. I know it, and I have allowed it to know me.

But I find in my Parisian estrangement a source of comfort I had not anticipated. I am free from too much involvement.

August

They write from Warsaw:

I feel that our life here isn't worth describing, just as it isn't worth describing life in a hospital. We are aware of the exclusive and distinctive nature of our life. We know that neither our sorrows nor our humor are worth telling. It can't be helped; after a year and a half of absence, you are now from "there," the two of you are no longer patients in this hospital and won't be amused by stories about the peculiar habits of our nurses and doctors, or about who's feeling better or feeling worse, who's going home and who has had to come back.

//

New clippings from the official weeklies published in Poland. In one of them I read: "By constantly creating the impression of omnipotence and unlimited possibilities, these people want to convince the public that they can smash or destroy at will. Hence many enlightened people are afraid to express their own opinion. That fear, in many cases, has a solid justification. Take the case of Zdzislaw Najder or Kazimierz Brandys. Both extremely influential. They did, in fact (and, after all, they are only a small chip off a big block) have the means necessary to make others act."

In the same article signed with a pseudonym, there is the following passage: "It now becomes understandable why revisionists and sneering critics cannot (or don't want to, which comes to the same) understand what such poets as Rej, Kochanowski, Slowacki, Mickiewicz, Wyspianski, Kasprowicz, Tetmajer, Broniewski, Czernik, or Grochowiak, mean to the Poles. They cannot understand it because those writers glorify permanent values rather than what happens to be fashionable in the marketplace."

Taking into consideration the tactical ingenuity of the ruling elite of the military and the police—which includes some pretty clever individuals—these quotations are striking for their combination of incredible stupidity and fear of an imagined power.

//

Sunday. Dinner and conversation. The heat is oppressive. Our hostess has very definite views on everything. Her husband perspires, sadly and silently. Two monologists sit across from each other, with their eyebrows raised, their noses thrust forward. One waits for the moment when the other will put a piece of meat in his mouth. The rest of the guests are bleary eyed; the hostess's husband has taken off his glasses and is wiping them with his napkin. It is hot. My feet are slowly beginning to swell inside my shoes. Somebody is talking about someone who has become a political whore. The hostess has very categorical opinions and large, busy lips. The first monologist cuts in when the second takes a breath, to begin his own *bel canto*. The second sinks into depression. My tie has turned limp. Why don't they serve water? What sins have we committed to deserve such punishment? The hostess's husband looks twenty years older. Ah, these small social tortures . . .

It is past midnight when I finally find myself outside. A taxi pulls up. Sitting behind the wheel is a young woman, smoking a cigarette: a man's shirt with rolled-up sleeves, fingers with pink-polished fingernails around the wheel. Next to her, curled up on a white fur blanket, a small greyhound in a diamond collar. The smell of Gauloise cigarettes and music on the radio: *"Si tu n'existais pas, je t'aurais inventée."* We glide past the Louvre. The woman speaks to the dog; I notice her profile, the narrow forehead, the shiny copper hair pushed back. I have the insane idea to put myself totally in her hands, which she probably guesses, because she turns around with a half smile. . . . "Thirty-two francs. Plus tip."

Certain women, caught only in a gesture or glance, and never seen again, can linger in your memory. Beautiful and mute, like paintings. There may be five or six of them in the course of your life, the women with enigmatic smiles, or the serious, self-involved women. Why can't they be forgotten? It is easier to dismiss from memory the women you have loved. The scarcely known women are eternal. Time brings them even closer, makes them more real. I remember one, with her blond braid and butterfly-shaped ribbon. She was throwing a bright *cerceau* ring into the air. And I remember another one, years later: She dipped a tin cup into a pail of water that stood on a stone wall surrounding the well, and, watching me drink the water in one quick gulp, she asked if I would like to come inside and rest. I can still see the lighter suntan line on her forehead just under the edge of her peasant kerchief and the tiny drops of perspiration over her upper lip. In front of me was the road leading to the cemetery. Walking with my bicycle to the gate, I stopped and turned around to look back. She was observing me with curious attention as she stood there by the well, her arm reaching behind her head, maybe adjusting the knot in her kerchief. I could see the lighter skin under her arm. I am not sure if she wore any shoes or sandals; I think she may have been barefoot. Neither am I certain that she was indeed looking at me; she may have been interested in my bicycle. Two hours later, on my way back, I noticed a man working by the well, repairing a plow.

I couldn't say today whether she was indeed as beautiful as I have remembered her, but I am thinking about her more and more often and more and more eagerly, and these moments have grown increasingly longer. Oddly enough, this has turned out to be one of the most important scenes from my past.

There are phenomena, encountered many years by the imagination, which continue to recur in life and are forever a source of wonder, even if literature has discarded them. What's happened to love? It is rarely the subject of contemporary novels, and when it is a theme, it is only as a symptom of the general degradation of the novel. In recent American prose, love has become a mixture of neurosis, sex, and horror, a tale of the mutual destruction of two people possessed by their own and by global madness. Recently, there has been a certain trend in the American novel to show eroticism in the convulsions of totalitarian holocaust (Fuentes has described it quite aptly as "imported agonies"), where artistic refinement would reach its pinnacle in a description of copulation in a gas chamber.

///

I read less here than I did in Warsaw: I walk around the city, ride the metro, meet people. Stefan Kisielewski is visiting here from Poland. He looked at me and said, "Gray hair becomes you." He himself hasn't changed at all. I inquired about his life in Warsaw. "It's not bad. I enjoy that kind of thing. I enjoyed the Stalinist period as well. I've always liked foreign occupation." He and I met in 1940. We used to have dinners together at an inexpensive restaurant catering to writers on Foksal Street. At that time we had both taken up writing novels. After the war, we both began publishing, I in *Kuznica*, he in *Tygodnik Powszechny*. Now Kisiel announces he's read my *Diary*. "I'm opposed to it. You lie on the sofa, you stare at the ceiling, you moan and groan. What's the use of it?" Again he looks at me, a bit sarcastically, with curiosity, and I like him anyway. Afterward, we watch the world track championship competitions in Helsinki on TV and see a Pole, Maminski, win a silver medal in the three-thousand-meter obstacle race. I take the bus home and then walk across the Tournelle Bridge. After dinner, I read *The Yellow Dog* by Simenon, alternately with *Lenin in Switzerland* by Solzhenitsyn, and I go to bed early. At five in the morning, buses start cruising up the street. The windows vibrate. I have two hours left until seven, enough time to reach the conclusion that in everything that Kisiel has said there is considerable truth, which consists in not taking history very seriously. This distinguishes him from most Poles, who take history seriously. Kisielewski is totally casual about it and even seems to find its macabre stupidities amusing. Which is why he can maintain with sincerity that he has enjoyed foreign occupation and the Stalinist period. They stimulate and entertain him. As we were parting, he said, "So, when're you coming back? We will elect you right away to something or other. . . ." And he eyed me playfully.

//

During the war, after my father died and I was living with my mother at a friend's house on Narbutta Street, at night I would often be seized by fear when I couldn't hear her breathe. I would ask whether she was asleep. She would not reply, but a moment later I would hear her sigh. She said she couldn't sleep because she was counting everything from the beginning. "Just think of all the things that've happened. . . ." There was infinite astonishment in her whisper. Something must have been missing in her summary. Maybe she couldn't find the common denominator to which the number of calamities could be reduced. She only kept repeating, "Just think, just think . . ." She was a woman of sound mind, and rather innocent. I suppose that in all of her life she had never been suspicious of the world. Today I think of what she must have been feeling then, in the middle of the night, over-whelmed by the astounding discovery that behind her fa-miliar, domestic existence, the knives were being sharpened. She wouldn't know how to define, to name, that discovery. I already knew. I knew what to expect; my instinct was warning me.

In 1939, I refused to leave Warsaw and travel East; a year later, I did not go behind the wall. I was being driven by a constant impulse: to cover up my traces. By the end of the war I was living in hiding. I surfaced in the winter, when the Ogre was being finished off, and I ran, shouting, stumbling in the snow, pointing my finger at the shiny airplanes high in the frigid sky. I felt safe and free. Where was I running? Across a village. I was the only person who ran across the village shouting with happiness. Our peasant host was chopping firewood when I came running into the barnyard. He turned around slowly and, taking a measured aim at a log with his ax, asked me if I had matches. Clearly this ponderous, phlegmatic man understood much better than I that there was no reason to hurry.

I think of that moment with embarrassment. Instead of coming into the open, maybe I should've been looking for an even safer hiding place.

//

A man I know has an evil personality. I shall try to describe his main characteristics.

He is dogmatic and forces his opinions on those around him. When confronted with the truth, he becomes furious. He won't hesitate to tell vulgar lies in order to discredit his opponent.

He is concerned, above all, with his prestige. He is vengeful and systematically destroys those who have displeased him. He holds those who are weaker in contempt. He thinks that people with principles are idiots.

When he wants to deceive, he can be crafty and hypocritical. He utters words he doesn't believe. He won't keep his promises, but will carry out all of his threats. He is noted for his relentlessness in destroying people who haven't met his demands. To make them obey, he diligently collects the facts from their past.

In work, he is unprofessional. He covers up his indolence and lack of qualifications with evasive prattle, or shifts the burden of responsibility to others. He won't accept advice, but listens to flattery. He is scared of his boss and distrustful of his subordinates. The thought that they may chew him out terrifies him. Then he becomes dangerous, capable of intrigue and blackmail. But he will not attack if there is risk involved. He knows how to wait for the right moment, and then acts with brutality.

Everyone is sick of him. The very sight of him and the sound of his voice are repugnant. But there isn't any way to get rid of him, since he has the support of the boss. Those who have attempted to expose him have lost their jobs. The rest are helpless. The man is really impossible.

If only this were just a man . . . but it is a country. For forty years it has been a political system and a government. The police and the army guarantee its impunity, press and television multiply its ugliness. By now, it has destroyed almost everything. People compare it to a spider, a plague, to a cancer that eats the body. There is no cure for it and no way out of it. Ultimately, one can only hate it.

It is, then, a life dominated by hate. Multiplied by endless, tedious days, dragging out for years. Is that anything to recommend to the young generation? I wonder about the wisdom of giving them any recommendations anyway; it is probably best to keep quiet. Let us imagine, however, that a student from Poland comes to me asking what he should do, how he should live. I could, naturally, dodge the question by saying that I myself had never asked a question such as this, or that one must find one's own answers, etc. And probably, after he was gone, it would occur to me that I might have, after all, told him one particular story. For there is a way to cope with reality by pushing it aside to a distant plane, and isolating yourself from it with a protective shield that makes survival possible (in medicine, the term "antibiotic shield" is sometimes used). It is a shield against the foreign life that has invaded us from without. I could tell him the story of a writer of fables.

The fables writer came from a cultured, assimilated Polish-Jewish family, and therefore, during the years of the German occupation, came under the so-called Aryan paragraph. When I asked him how he managed to live in those days, he looked at me with his kindly eyes of a sybarite and said, "Very simply. The German occupation didn't affect me. I was in love." The day that Paris fell, he swallowed poison, because the woman he loved told him she loved someone else. The day that the Germans surrendered at Stalingrad, he walked into a bar on Nowy Swiat and saw her seated at one of the tables; he fell to his knees, and then fainted. She therefore agreed to meet him, but only to tell him once again that she would not leave her husband. The fables writer began losing weight rapidly, and it only brought out his Semitic features. He was eating mostly sweets. One day, while he went to buy a "mocha" tart in one of the cafés, two plainclothesmen approached him. He followed them to the Szucha Alley (Gestapo headquarters), where two men in uniform showered him with abuse, shouting he was a Jew. To which the fables writer quietly replied that they were mistaken, but that if they wished, they were welcome to shoot him, because he wasn't interested in staying alive. When, obviously taken aback, they asked him why, he explained, "The woman I love doesn't want to be with me, and life without her is worthless to me." Whereupon the two men in uniform burst out laughing and threw him out. The fables writer walked downstairs, but stopped at the entrance by the sentry stand, since he had just remembered he left his "mocha" tart upstairs. So he walked up again, all the way to the third floor, knocked on the door, excused himself, and took his tart. But he continued losing weight, because he was in love. He didn't win his beloved woman until after the war. He started having affairs soon after they were married. It was a good marriage, lasting until the fables writer's death.

Another writer I know was in love with a woman from 1948 until 1953, that is to say from the moment of the liquidation of the opportunistic rightist deviation until the funeral of Joseph Stalin. It was, as he said, love as necessary defense, an antidote to the ideology to which he, regrettably, had succumbed. Fifteen years later, he fell in love again, also in a politically tense situation; the year was 1968. In both cases, his love subsided during the brief periods of liberalization.

Such stories from the past somehow come back to you in the middle of August, when your brain is exhausted from the heat. But it has turned cooler in the last few days. Autumn is upon us.

///

Of the thirteen imprisoned Solidarity and KOR leaders, I knew Michnik best, and this is why the thought of him in a prison cell is so hard for me to accept. He does not seem to have much physical resistance. I doubt if his health is robust, and I remember worrying about him when he would come to visit me in the winter dressed in a light, skimpy windbreaker, his hands ice cold. Neither his temperament nor his style of living predisposed him for prison life. He insisted with sincerity that he was scared. He often said so to the women he liked. He led a socially active, busy life, surrounded by friends and women, between parties and political discussions, as if trying to take advantage of his freedom and love of life, which he was ready at any moment to give up. From time to time, he would disappear: arrested. Periodically, he would go into retreat at the Laski Institute for the Blind in order to write. M. had once witnessed his conversation with one of the Laski nuns. Adam was encouraging her strongly to read Shestov, and the sister said, blushing, that no, thank God she didn't know Russian. Michnik stuttered with indignation. "Wha . . . what are you t . . . telling me, s . . . sister! There's only one shepherd and one fold!" I had never met anyone like him before. I saw him often. He would visit

me on Nowomiejska Street. We talked about politics, literature, all things on earth and in heaven. When he left, in his
wake would be ashtrays full of cigarette stubs, a crumpled
rug under the chair in which he had sat, and an unfinished
cup of coffee. He always moved and intrigued me.

Michnik represented something new. He was different,
and also different from me, probably in the degree of his
intensity. He lived impulsively, yet he was also rational and
sober in his convictions. But I and others like me, lived at
peace with our convictions, whereas he could not. He simply
didn't seem capable of settling down, because he could not
reconcile himself to the discrepancies between the actual
world and his ideals.

//

In Poland all has been transformed. You can say that the
right is still the right, and the left, the left, but what does
it really mean, since we now have workers' councils that
combine the cult of the Virgin Mary with syndicalist demands,
neoconservative groups animated by the spirit of reform, and
liberal atheistic circles influenced by ideas of the Dominican
order? Catholicism is different, nationalism has become something else, socialism is no longer Marxist, rationalism has
begun to take into account the existence of God.

//

We decided to go and see a film being shown at a small
cinema on Monsieur-le-Prince Street. We arrived a bit too

early, and the ticket booth was still closed. M. suggested we try to find the hotel we had lived in for two months during our first stay in Paris in 1946. So, we walk slowly down the street. Our hotel must have changed its name; the owner inquires whether we would like to rent a room. That isn't it. There was a different entrance. I remember that immediately to the right was the room of the doorman, a young Arab. When we would come home late at night and ring the doorbell, the Arab would let us in, and as we passed the half-open door to his little room, we could see the owner's wife asleep in his bed. The forty-year-old woman's husband always went fishing the latter part of the week.

The name of the hotel did not change; from a distance we can see the vertical sign reading UNIVERS. Across the street, a Chinese restaurant. We walked here, thirty-seven years ago, thirty-seven years younger.

We have been walking, as we are now, for half a century. After school, I'd run to Marszalkowska Street to wait inside the front entrance of a house on the corner of Wspolna Street, and as M. approached I would suddenly appear, as if out of nowhere. We would both fake surprise, she would switch her briefcase to the other hand, and I remember her startled smile. "What a pleasant surprise . . ." I would inquire cordially whether I might be allowed to walk her home.

We have been fortunate. We have come full circle. We realize that there is nothing wiser or better than our own youthful conception of the world, with its funny distinction between good and evil. We stood staring at Monsieur-le-

Prince Street as if it were a flowing river, trying to see some reflection of days long gone, of old scenes, and faces. For a moment we tried imagining ourselves as we were then. In such moments you feel envy, a touch of pity, and you get nowhere. We went to the movies.

The show consisted of newsreels from 1900 to 1940. It showed crowds in the streets, horse-drawn trolleys, political strikes and demonstrations, opera premieres, balls, cities on the day that the war broke out, and bombs falling.

//

I have just read a report written by a foreigner who had taken a trip to Poland. Customs officials had confiscated all of his notes and books. When he returned home, he wrote down his impressions. I shall quote a few passages:

The Poles are lively people, like the southerners, but they haven't had a Machiavellian education and lack political wisdom. It's a nation whom Napoleon had no trouble convincing that their legions must shed blood for him . . . it was enough for him to wave the white eagle in front of their noses . . . This kind of youthful or childish enthusiasm is most certainly not a stabilizing element in view of the giant struggles of all nations for survival in an era of industrialization and militarism. It is not compatible with good management, cleverness, discipline, moderation. . . . Historical descriptions of the Poles seem to emphasize the fact that they can always be counted on for gallantry and personal courage, but claim that there is a certain conceit in their high-mindedness, something capricious in their magnanimous nature; that they are stubborn,

quick to quarrel, contentious, unable to accept any rule or regu-
lation outside of their own will, incapable of concentrating on any
particular goal. . . . In sum, they display a mixture of Western
and Eastern faults. . . . When asked, in a large group, what I
thought, as a critic, of Polish society, I replied without hesitation,
"You are a nation of dilettantes." It seems that this definition, in
its broadest meaning, is correct, but we must not forget why the
Poles are as they are. We must never lose sight of the fact that
these are people with a great deal of natural energy and no chance
to give vent to that energy . . . people with a spirited, indomitable
flair for politics, who have been denied any political education,
having been forbidden to elect their own representatives or make
decisions in matters of national significance . . . one must always
remember the nation that, from the dawn of history, has enthu-
siastically defended the rights of the individual, but today is forced
to live without any legal protection from the abuses of random
officials. . . . "Life in Warsaw," said one of the most prominent
men in town to me, "is full of nervous tension; in the long run,
it is unbearable. . . ." We are confronted with a people whose
nerves are strained to the point of breaking, for they must struggle
day after day for their very existence. A people totally consumed
by problems of national survival—and, after all, national survival
is a universal problem, embracing all of mankind.

These words were written in 1885. "Impressions from
Poland" appeared in the most recent issue of *Zeszyty Histo-
ryczne* (*Historical Notebooks*), published by the Polish Literary
Institute in Paris. The author, Georg Brandes, was born in
1842 and died in 1927. He was a thinker, a writer, an essayist,

one of the most illustrious figures in Danish literary life. He had visited Poland twice.

//

Why is the Arc de Triomphe in Paris more impressive than the Empire State Building in New York? Because of the perspective afforded by its location? Because it symbolizes a grander epoch, or is more magnificent?

It *is* magnificent. But its magnificence consists mostly in its masterful staging. Paris is the work of architects who used space to reconstruct history. *Arc de Triomphe—Concorde—Tuileries—Louvre. Arc de Triomphe—Défense.* When facing southwest, you see a perspective encompassing the Empire period, the Directory, the site of the guillotine, the Bourbons, and the night of Saint Bartholomew. If you face northwest, you see a group of modern Défense skyscrapers that after dusk light up like a computer screen. Toward the arc from nine directions are boulevards, all named for great leaders and famous battles (and also one writer). The arc can be variously appreciated from different angles; at close range it shines like limestone. It is inspiring. The arc brings together various epochs. It is magnificent because it is at the center of France's history.

Concord Square—Square of the Star—Avenue of the Great Army—District of Defense. The pathos of French rhetoric has always originated from energy of thought and action. Nowadays France is tired, like a man who has experienced all that he has wanted to experience and now prefers to be left in peace. His energy has been used up. Poland is tired for the opposite reason: like a man whose energy has not been exhausted and who has not experienced what he has wanted to experience. He too may prefer to be left in peace.

How would the Danish critic Georg Brandes describe Warsaw a hundred years later, in the autumn of 1983? Probably as follows:

Poland is presently the only country in the Soviet empire where Roman Catholic mass is attended by huge crowds; where illegal antigovernment books and publications are widely read; where the leader of the opposition, considered by the majority of the population to be the leader of the country, is a free man, makes speeches and gives interviews; where the true monarch—the Pope—is cheered in the streets by millions; where next to official government buildings, an underground committee conducts its clandestine activities. In this country, lacking any authentic public institutions, people live expecting help from God.

Brandes might notice the main artery running through the city representing three hundred years of Poland's history— from the Royal Palace and the column from the Waza period, up Krakowskie Przedmiescie with all its churches, past the Association for the Promotion of Science and the building out of which Chopin's piano was thrown to the pavement, down to the Belveder Palace and the Soviet Embassy. He might be struck by the fact that from time to time the artery loses its continuity: In some places it runs between medium-sized, two- and three-story buildings. He might observe that it was modest, less planned than its equivalents in other capitals. He explains it this way: the Poles haven't had a powerful monarchy or a rich bourgeoisie, or the momentum of a great civilization; a few magnates' residences and churches were erected, then came the partitions, poverty, and very little business activity. What might surprise him most, would be the fact that a long stretch of the city, destroyed during the war, has been carefully and lovingly rebuilt. He might wonder: Has it been worth it? In which case he would not have understood one important thing: that the rebuilding of the city, the reconstruction of the past, has been the country's last successful undertaking, and that after this common effort nothing else that the country had wanted has been achieved.

Walesa was nowhere to be found when the news that he had won the Nobel Peace Prize arrived. Early that morning he had gone to the woods to gather mushrooms.

December

"God, grant me indifference toward that which I cannot change, courage to change what can be changed, and wisdom to distinguish one from the other."

This sentence was written by a wise man whose name I shall not reveal, just to make life difficult for the erudites. I repeated this sentence to myself as I walked down Arago Boulevard. It was a bright day, gold-and-red leaves rustled on the sidewalks. I walked with the help of my cane along the empty boulevard. The Arago Boulevard isn't beautiful, but I felt quite cheerful. That day I had a doctor's appointment at the Cochin hospital. The head medical man in the rheumatology division is Professor Amor, the doctor's name is

Illouze. I found both names rather appealing. Love and illusion . . . Professor Love and Dr. Illusion. I had never been treated by specialists of this kind. After a month of arguments, I had given M. permission to telephone the hospital to set up an appointment, and now I was walking there, happy at the thought that in an hour it would all be over. I stopped a nun in a white habit, who was walking her bicycle, to ask for directions. She smiled a friendly smile, showing her long teeth. "At the corner you will turn left, and the hospital is right there." She spoke with an English accent. I turned left.

I had managed to ignore my illness and had gotten used to living with it. But in New York my condition had worsened. To get up from a chair I now had to support myself with both hands; crossing the street I had to be careful to measure my steps so as to reach the opposite sidewalk with my left foot, because with the right I have trouble stepping up. And both my legs . . .

I didn't finish the last sentence. I should've omitted the entire passage, but I am leaving it in for the record. Or rather, as a warning: A thought, barely begun, may not want to live longer. I've decided not to dispose of the body. Let it remain. Let it always serve as a reminder that, when writing, one is never safe.

//

The future is frightening. The West is afraid of war. Actually, what does it matter if I'm devoured by the Russia of the czars or the Soviet Union—or maybe it's pointless to ponder such things anyway. But somehow I persist, as if the fate of the world depended on it. Every evening I plant myself in front of the television set; the attractive newswoman, Mademoiselle Christine Ockrent, tells me all about the contemporary world. A world filled with armaments, hate, and savage faces. From time to time, there's news from Poland: Butter is rationed again, Walesa has met with the underground Solidarity leaders, women wearing their hand-knit wool caps stand in line in front of a store on Marszalkowska Street. I stare at the wide screen. The pretty Mademoiselle Ockrent now talks about Lebanon: demolished houses and screaming mothers with babies in their arms. God, don't let me become indifferent toward things I cannot change. When it turns chilly in our apartment, the two of us sit together in front of the television set, bundled up in blankets. Television has become the image of the world for us. We don't know the will of God. Every evening we wait with nervous anticipation. We have a deep need for good news.

Our waiting is naive, and our faith meager.

//

Copies of the American edition of *Miesiace*, translated by Richard Lourie, have just arrived. The title: *A Warsaw Diary*. On the back cover, comments about the book by Philip Roth, Milan Kundera, Irwing Howe, and Zbigniew Brzezinski. By separate mail, I received a copy with a note from Klara

Glowczewski, my American editor. I wrote back: "It is less likely that this book will be a success than that the Empire State Building will turn over and stand upside down."

//

A long evening walk through Montparnasse. Dry air with a hint of smoke, warm lights, and the smell of roasted chestnuts. Behind a restaurant's window, people sit at tables, a gravy-dish sparkles, somebody's hand lifts a glass of wine, a cuff link in a narrow, white cuff, and a waiter bent over a table. This picture, except for some brief interruptions, hasn't changed for at least a century and a half. The land of enchantment, the dream of normal living, where Hansel and Gretel are wandering around, frightened by the wolf.

The Polish word *niewola* cannot be easily translated into French. *Captivité? Dépendance? Asservissement? Soumission nationale?* . . . No. *Esclavage?* Definitely not. It is similar to the English *slavery*. None of the words apply; it too means something else. Kundera suggests it would be a good idea to introduce the term *nonliberté*. I point out to him that the word *niewola* also connotes *nonvolonté*.

//

When Western intellectuals try to teach us what Russia used to be and no longer is, I am reminded of an answer once given to a literary critic. During a discussion at the end of Wiech's literary soirée at the Polish Writers' Union, critic L. accused Wiech of lacking a sense of humor. Wiech took the floor: "In connection with the critical remark made by my colleague L., I would like to tell a story about Baron Rothschild. He was having breakfast on the Champs Elysées when a beggar approached him, insisting he must give him money. 'My good man,' said Rothschild quite annoyed, 'here are five francs, but in the future you must remember never to annoy people by begging while they eat.' 'Mr. Rothschild,' answered the beggar, 'you may be a great banker, but you'll not teach me how to beg.' "

//

M. is in the kitchen; the radio is on. I am puttering around my room. I listen, then go to the kitchen and find her standing motionless. Both of us stare at the radio. News from Poland: the head of the KGB has come to Warsaw with a delegation (we didn't catch his name). Western correspondents claim that the key government positions in the Polish People's Republic are to be filled by Soviet advisors.

//

I am taping my final program for Radio France Internationale before taking a long-planned break. I have chosen to read a passage from the Diary about a winter evening on Nowy Swiat—the memories of my school days. I am reading about horse-drawn sleighs coming down the street, about dorozkas and gentlemen in bowler hats, a window display in a fashionable shop, and a grocery store with pheasants and a dead rabbit hanging on the wall. I try to convey to my listeners the flavor of that prewar scene in Warsaw, and I tell them in conclusion that this represents the safest period of my life. Then we replay the recorded text. I hear myself: . . . "represents the safest period of my life," and think, what am I saying?

//

Yesterday, while walking, I stopped at a square some distance from a church. The square was hemmed in by a low fence with a small gate; a group of noisy students sat on a bench; one of the boys was eating a sandwich, throwing the crumbs to the sparrows. Overhead, a few clouds, chestnut tree branches, and an overall aura of peace. It was a scene from half a century ago, permeated with peace from half a century ago. After school we always went to the square next to the Evangelical Church. The square was bordered by trees; you entered it through a small gate. We would sit on a bench, inside a kind of arbor. I may add that we were still quite innocent as far as humanity was concerned, and our consciousness was not yet cluttered by piles of corpses and lies. We didn't discuss Hitler or Stalin, but rather Oskar Bartel, our class supervisor and history teacher, whom we liked a lot. Sometimes we mulled over the fascinating case of our geography teacher, Professor Ballawelder, who was preparing for seven years to take a trip to Africa (money was being collected by the students to buy equipment for the trip), and, having taken all the shots against tropical diseases, went to the station, accompanied by students and the entire staff, and, as the train pulled out to the sound of enthusiastic cries of farewell, a large suitcase fell off the shelf, hitting Professor Ballawelder on the head; luckily, two days later he woke up inside the hospital of Infant Jesus, but never did get to see Africa. It was a famous story. We repeated it, sad, but delighted, huddled close together on our bench, our school bags between our knees. We wore navy-blue cloth caps, and sometimes out of boredom we would toss them at a flock of sparrows. If I were to paint that picture today, I would put in the background, in the tree branches behind us, or above our heads, the sneering beasts and monstrous creatures with the snouts of Notre Dame gargoyles, or the horned riders of Lebenstein's stained glass windows.

//

"Boy, what is the matter?", Professor Bartel asked me one winter after our first lesson. I had come to school pale from lack of sleep, and not entirely conscious. During the morning classes in the winter, the lights would be turned on, and the light bothered my eyes. Bartel looked at me carefully. "Chin up, my boy," and he walked away quickly in the direction of the teachers' room. Most of the time, however, he treated us with sarcastic mockery, which we were quite broad minded about. If he came to class without a smirk on his face, we knew that his wife wasn't feeling well that day.

During the war, I met him only once, at the beginning of 1940, soon after we left our apartment on Asnyk Street. It had been taken over by Liebert, the director of *Arbeitsamt*,

who was later executed by the Home Army. We were told
to move out that same day. My mother packed three suitcases,
the superintendent stored all our paintings (M. and I sold
them later, up until the end of the war), we managed to find
a room on Filtrowa Street to sublease from the wife of a
colonel fighting with the Polish Army in France. After spending the night on a little side sofa, I went with my father to
see the administrator of the house. The thin little man in
glasses rose from his chair and announced he would not
register us as tenants. "You'll have to look for a room elsewhere." The news of our eviction from our house on Asnyk
Street must have already reached him. He pushed our iden-
tification papers aside. My father's upper lip trembled, his
face turned red. "It's your duty to . . ." "I will not accept
your application," repeated the administrator, "it's forbidden." He was lying. So far, nothing of this sort had been
announced; he got the lead on the German decree issued for
the Jewish quarter. I wanted to say this to him, but my father
caught me by the arm. He started to shout. His shouting
was terrifying. Five thousand years of pain suddenly came to
the surface in this big, self-confident man. He shouted about
barbarians and savages. He screamed about Einstein, about
the mother of Jesus! I ran after him into the street, several
people stopped to look at us. As I was trying to calm him
down, I suddenly noticed Oskar Bartel walking out of the
teachers' cooperative building next door. My father rushed
toward him. He called, "Professor, will you believe this!
. . . Professor! . . ." He was breathless, panting. I quickly

explained what had happened. Bartel stood there, looking very tired, with a suffering expression on his face. I too felt uneasy. His wife was Jewish, I had been told one day during a recess by Jurek Lichtenstein.

///

Dr. Illouse saw me precisely at eleven. He made me lie flat on my back and, twisting my bent knees, asked me whether I was Polish. Then a nurse came in to warn the doctor that his next patient smelled of cat urine. The man who was sitting next to me in the waiting room did emit a strong odor; he told the woman who sat on his left that he had had an onslaught of arthritis, but was now feeling much better thanks to the warmth of cats' fur. "He has eleven cats who all sleep in his bed," said the nurse. While the doctor was writing my prescription, I inquired about the causes of my own ailment. "The causes are a complete mystery," said Dr. Illouse. "Arthritis strikes for unknown reasons and the cure for it is also unknown." Indocid 75 comes in big capsules; you take one at breakfast, then chew two Lyophos tablets during the day against side effects. Sleeping with cats might make me feel better, because Indocid obviously doesn't cure arthritis; it only lessens the pain. But the capsule made it possible for me to get home before the torrential rain washed the light off the walls on Saint Anthony's Street.

January 1984

Order reigned in Warsaw. Despite appeals by the underground Temporary Coordinating Commission (TKK), people
didn't take to the streets. There was no march through the
city, no protesting crowd. I hear: "They were weary, didn't
think it would serve any purpose." Or these bitter words:
"They could've walked on the sidewalks . . ."

I'm not sure how I would have acted if I had been in
Warsaw on December 16. Probably like the others. I cannot
evaluate from afar the significance or the causes of the lack
of response. If I were in Warsaw, I'd probably know more.
Or maybe not. Maybe they themselves were surprised by

what happened and don't really understand it. Mass responses
are sometimes difficult to predict.

//

N. has come for a visit, and brought some copies of underground newspapers smuggled out of Poland, along with stacks
of official magazines. She claims that at present the illegal
newspapers have a greatly diminished circulation. They reach
only small segments of society, mostly the academic circles,
and are published in very limited editions. But they are
important. They build a bond, develop character and judgment, offer a glimmer of authenticity. Among the magazines
brought by N., the legal ones, was a copy of *Radar*, the weekly
of "creative work," as its printed subtitle informs. In the
issue I find a quotation from a speech by the Minister of
Internal Affairs, presented during a session of the *Sejm* (Polish
Parliament) ("Certain alien circles, in trying to create more
tension inside Poland, are applying the well-known, histor-
ically proven method: with the help of Poles against Poland"),
and a statement by the Secretary of the Central Committee,
Swirgon ("The primary aim of our operations is to socialize
the decision making in film production.") In addition, some
information about prices of books sold outside of the
bookstores.

In official propaganda, there's cynicism and gibberish; in
the marketplace, there's a frantic push toward anything with
value, even dubious value. Not only are prices horrendously
steep but for many years some of the most important books

have been unavailable—those you need in the beginning, as well as those you cannot do without later. They are called mental nourishment. Or they used to be called that. The result of it will probably be felt in five, in twenty years, or maybe even today. N. said to me, "After coming here, after three days of reading the press and looking at television, you're suddenly bombarded by thoughts."

//

Antenne 2 has broadcast an interview from Warsaw with Zbigniew Bujak, member of the TKK of underground Solidarity. Bujak had been in hiding for twenty-five months. He was disguised, in a wig and a fake beard. His room had practically no furniture, one table, a chair, a sleeping mat on the floor. Through the window you could see rows of gray buildings. Bujak calmly described life conditions in the underground. He demonstrated some technical details, such as a method of corresponding by way of tiny, easy to swallow paper rolls. He said that he had managed twice to escape from his hiding place just before the arrival of the police, and that once he was arrested accidentally, but was able to get away. When asked whether he intended to come out of hiding, he replied, "No, to give up resistance would be a mistake, as the Czech example clearly shows us." He spoke without gloating, very simply; one didn't sense any nervous tension. He showed his small television set, which he turns on for the last ten minutes of every news broadcast. "Because that's when they announce who has been arrested, or who has come out of hiding . . ." At the end of the interview, he lay on his mat, with a book on the floor next to him. He said a few words about literature, that it could never be destroyed. The interview had been taped before December 16. The fact that the TKK's appeals for protests in the streets received no response, the significance of which is not yet fully realized, has deepened the prisoners' isolation and made them feel unnecessary. Watching that television interview, I wondered what this man in the clumsy wig will do next? Will he still want to, and can he, remain in hiding?

///

An evening at the Chojeckis' on *Tolbiac*. The telephone rings every few minutes. London calling. Chojecki, squatting, answers in monosyllables, then makes notes in his calendar. The conversation is brief, but immediately the telephone rings again. Brussels calling. All this makes talking rather difficult. We have been discussing Adam Michnik's letter to the Minister of the Interior. A copy of the letter had reached Paris on Christmas Eve. On the day after Christmas we were invited to Maisons-Laffitte (the publishers of the monthly *Kultura*), where, before a festive lunch, they played the tape with the recorded text of the letter. On a glassed-in veranda, thirty people were seated around a large table. Next to me, Lebenstein, then M., Jelenski, Herling-Grudzinski and his wife, the daughter of Benedetto Croce; over to the left, Mrozek and the Skalmowskis, Teresa Dzieduszycka and Zenon Modzelewski, the father superior of the Pallotine monks. Across the table from me sat Jerzy Giedroyc, gray, erect, his head practically motionless, a miniature anchor pinned in the lapel of his blue blazer; to his left, Chojecki. Jozef Czapski came down later and joined us for a short time. What struck me about Adam's letter was its impetuous tone. It was a reply to a suggestion that he should leave Poland. They took away Michnik's books and kept him in a prison cell with criminals. He had issued a protest, to which an answer came from General Kiszczak. The Minister of Internal Affairs offered the prisoner freedom in exchange for his consent to leave the country. "You could spend your holidays at the *Côte d'Azur* . . ." In his letter, Michnik refuses the offer, using very strong language. You can detect in it genuine rage, which I interpreted as wounded pride, or maybe the desperation that comes from rejecting temptation. Up until then, Michnik's articles and letters sent from prison haven't had such a violent pitch.

The Chojeckis drove us back to Paris. In a basket on the backseat slept their one-month-old son, whom they had given the double name of Jacek-Adam. As we were driving and talking about the letter, Chojecki kept silent. I felt that this was perhaps a difficult moment for him and he would rather be in prison with Adam on Rakowiecka Street. But yesterday he spoke up during dinner. After one of his numerous telephone calls, he mentioned that there was a rumor going around Warsaw about Michnik's letter being forged. Its text has been allegedly sent to embassies and foreign correspondents. However, some of Adam's friends maintain that his reply was genuine, but that he had allowed himself to become a victim of provocation. The authorities wanted very much to have in their possession, and to publicize, a letter from one of the leading KOR members rejecting an opportunity to emigrate, thus proving to this outside world that Polish authorities had acted in good faith and now had no choice but to proceed with the trial.

It's difficult to imagine that they would risk falsifying the letter. Michnik could easily have exposed the fraud. He probably wrote it in anger. They have probably achieved their goal.

The official manipulators think that Michnik is crazy, or a fool. They aren't the only ones who think that. For many people, his self-denial seems like a wasted heroic effort, even if, without knowing him, they speak of him as "little Adam." If he were convicted, they would soon forget him, only maybe now and then one of them would mutter over a glass of vodka something about heroes ending up in cemeteries.

///

In an old copy of *Letters to Madame Z.* that somebody sent me from Warsaw, I came across the following words: "To me, the intellectual measure of humanity in the period in which we live, is the conviction that the socialist forms of communal life are the only right ones." Clearly a wrong statement; I had written it in 1958. At that time, I think, it would have been accepted by some very prominent artists and scholars in the West, such as Picasso, Sartre, Buñuel, Fuentes, Yves Montand, as well as Jacques Monod and several other Nobel laureates. In 1958, Michnik was in his early teens and had just founded the Club of the Seekers of Contradiction. I have written earlier about the *state of error* in which I was living, I as well as others. I said that it was the closest thing to a state of religious faith. But it was also a rejection of faith and a turning away from ethical origins. Often in my conversations with Michnik, I maintained that moral disaster consists of a loss of access to oneself. In accepting communism, I was unable to make a moral and psychological effort to know myself. Myself as a person accepting communism. Inhibited not only by ideology but also by vanity, I did not dare to face the few essential motives in my thinking and writings. I didn't want to abandon my illusions and self-deception for inconvenient truths and I was unable to notice the source of the untruth in myself. Michnik, I suspect, understood all of this very well indeed, having grown up surrounded by this sort of thing, but above all he understood that there is no price that justifies abandoning certain principles of thought and action. Accordingly, he decided to go all the way, as did Kuron and Lipski, who voluntarily returned from London straight to prison, and as Vaclav Havel did to Prague. This is, presumably, a way to historical fame. I'm not too fond of thinking in these terms; Michnik didn't like it either. (He once joked, "I'm getting to be a Kościuszko".) I hope he won't be convicted and will soon be freed, along with the other ten prisoners. They have already achieved historical fame: Their freedom would only mean they did not have to pay too cruel a price for it.

///

Yesterday morning, a telephone call from Olga Scherer about the arrival of the Kijowskis. They have received their passports, after applying twice, and will be in Paris in ten days.

The themes and the specifics of our years in Warsaw seem more and more like a heavy, restless dream, the kind in which you toss and turn and pull at your blanket. New York and Paris are another dream, lighter and less realistic, of the sort occurring mostly in the second half of the night, or early morning. The odd thing is that characters appearing in the first dream can suddenly pop up in the second, simply move in, with all their luggage. I am wondering how it will feel to walk and talk again with the Kijowskis, and how in the world I can recapture that first dream's quick, playfully absurd language.

Kijowski was one of the three young Polish literature students studying in Kraków under Kazimierz Wyka, who were the first—soon after 1950—to pierce the balloon of postwar literature. They accused it of whitewashing and schematization. These terms gained instant wide acceptance. For thirty years, Kijowski followed the route of an outsider in the life of People's Poland; today he is nearest to the Catholic viewpoint. He has been an extremely keen observer, never totally committed, making comments from a distance, from the sidelines. I've always sensed in him a critical attitude toward the issues that excite me. He has written five times about my own books—three times favorably, twice without mercy. I believe that for a long time he didn't trust me, and then something seemed to thaw between us and we became friends. What interests me is that which sets us apart. I have in mind especially one serious difference: that he knew how to avoid the pitfalls which I got caught in voluntarily.

///

I am reading the text of an interview with a French intellectual, published in a highbrow periodical:

In the eighteenth and nineteenth centuries, an intense struggle between two different world views was taking place. On one side was the view proclaiming that human nature is basically good, that history represents progress . . . On the other side was the Catholic thought, decidedly pessimistic, unyielding, and free of illusions: Man is marked by original sin, contaminated by evil from the start. From the conception of man as being essentially good, from the image of nature not warped by the evil society (Marxism: the community, once it becomes liberated from class struggle, will find a luminous road to progress and happiness), or polluted by criminal blood (Nazism: the elimination of the racially foreign element will herald the arrival of the superman), come two of the greatest political, ideological, and moral disasters of the twentieth century. Here, then, is what rejecting the basic principles of the Judeo-Christian thought will lead to. The fact that all the avant-gardes of our century, at one time in history or another, have been partners of the two totalitarianisms, despite often being their first victims, never ceases to make one wonder.

In intellectual circles in this part of the world, this kind of language is heard more and more frequently. There has been a turning point: Today leftist elites are revising the basic elements of their faith. They seem to be going through what the Polish, Hungarian, and Czech intellectuals, committed to building socialist facades, went through twenty or thirty years ago. For the turning point to occur here, there had to be a *Gulag Archipelago*, an Afghanistan invasion, the outburst and suppression of Polish Solidarity. And also possibly the death of Jean-Paul Sartre. His funeral was attended by huge crowds; they were bidding farewell to a man who for forty years represented the intellectual conscience of the left. They honored him, knowing he had frequently been wrong. With him ended half a century of illusions; they were bidding farewell to their own past.

//

Why I am writing this in connection with Andrzej Kijowski, I can't explain. Though I feel I'm beginning to understand it. Maybe what has protected him against falling into a state of error was a childhood informed with a Catholic dread of sin, enabling him to resist an ideology that rejects mystery, whereas I was drawn to the rationalistic perspective of progress, free of the *sacrum*.

KAZIMIERZ BRANDYS was born in Lodz, Poland, and studied law at Warsaw University. His first novel was published in 1946, followed by nine others, a number of which have appeared in translation. He received the prestigious Italian Premio Elba Award in 1964, and his novel *Samson* was made into a film of the same title by director Andrzej Wajda. In 1966 Brandys resigned from the Polish Communist party, of which he had been a prominent member since 1946, and in 1978 cofounded *Zapis*, the renowned independent literary quarterly. He emigrated to New York in 1981. He now lives in Paris.